RACING
SYSTEMS WITH THE
POCKET CALCULATOR

RACING
SYSTEMS WITH THE
POCKET CALCULATOR

by John White

foulsham

LONDON • NEW YORK • TORONTO • SYDNEY

foulsham

The Publishing House, Bennetts Close,
Cippenham, Berkshire, SL1 5AP

ISBN 0-572-01789-8

Phototypeset in Great Britain by Typesetting Solutions, Slough, Berks.
Printed in Great Britain by St Edmundsbury Press Ltd,
Bury St Edmunds, Suffolk.

For all my family and
all my "racing" friends

About the author

In 1990 John White was voted Magazine Sportswriter of the Year. A past contributor to The Sporting Life Weekender, The Observer Colour Supplement, Competition Rider, Royalty Monthly, The Lady, the Irish Post, Equestrian World, Mensa, Writer's Monthly, The Betting Man's Contact and to Racing Monthly and Turf and Track as its systems expert, he has already published First Past the Post and Dark Secrets of the Turf — both compendiums of strategies for making racing far more profitable and enjoyable — as well as a complete encyclopedia of racing for Harper Collins.

Happy to combine journalism with examining and lecturing in English Literature, he lives close to one of his favourite tracks at Stratford-upon-Avon.

Acknowledgements

My debts to my wife and to my daughter Nicola for a very difficult piece of word-processing, to John Burford and to my father for checking the manuscript, and to Derek Payne for first getting me "button pressing", are all considerable.

Contents

'The one that got away'

Introduction

As Mark Twain so wisely said, it is the difference of opinion that makes horse racing and yet, because the initial opinion of many a backer is abandoned, winners are regularly missed. Self-recrimination is the inevitable upshot, as the "Sport of Kings", and of so many of their subjects, again proves too stern a test of character. Significantly though, those who fail the test, like anglers describing "the one that got away", often report how it would have been otherwise had they followed their initial inclinations.

The problem here lies not with Lady Luck, but with our fickle human nature. "Striving to better, oft we mar what's well" since, out of greed or in the emotional heat of the betting moment, we behave in ways which we later rue as near lunatic betrayals of our past convictions or lessons previously learnt the hard way.

One explanation for the changes of heart and mind to which backers prove so susceptible is that the betting forecast and, to an even greater extent, the actual course betting do a great deal to distort the initially quite dispassionate assessments of horses' winning chances that backers may engage in as they process the many non-financial (usually form-based) variables that so crucially influence the results of races.

'Thanks to the calculator'

For example, the lemming-like behaviour of many racegoers and betting-shop habitués in abandoning their initial fancies on rational selection criteria for "false" favourites or "springers" whose opening prices are massively trimmed is one major reason why, in bookmakers' parlance, the horse leading the market is known as "the jolly" and why those who blindly follow the money find the road to fortune is made up of losing distances.

Fortunately, though, thanks to the pocket calculator – today so widely available and used in a whole host of general, educational, scientific and commercial applications – the backer can acquire a "minder" to ensure that he or she does not, through sheer fickleness and lack of faith in initial form assessments, become his or her own worst enemy and the friend of bookmakers.

'High Risk'

CHAPTER 1

Calculating which races to work on

In its capacity as the "minder" of the backer, the pocket calculator should not be asked to offer protection against the dangers of operating in the high-risk area that a race with a large field represents. Thus, on any racing day, the backer should first discount all races which have more than 10 runners, not just because bookmakers are more likely to offer overall value for money when they are offering odds against a small number of runners, but because any effect the draw may have and the risk of interference in running are both likely to be reduced if a small field faces the starter.

The backer should start by calculating which race with a smallish field is the one least likely to produce a freak result. This, as long experience has shown, is often the race which carries the greatest prize money – perhaps one of the many "pattern" or "listed" races that are staged each season (which often tend to be won by horses with obvious claims on form and time) or a less prestigious non-handicap or rich handicap that has not attracted a large field.

Value of race to its winner in £ (its added or penalty value)	Rating to be entered into memory for race with 10 or fewer runners
100,001 or more	18
50,001 – 100,000	17
40,001 – 50,000	16
30,001 – 40,000	15
20,001 – 30,000	14
15,001 – 20,000	13
12,501 – 15,000	12
10,001 – 12,500	11
9,001 – 10,000	10
8,001 – 9,000	9
7,001 – 8,000	8
6,001 – 7,000	7
5,001 – 6,000	6
4,001 – 5,000	5
3,001 – 4,000	4
2,001 – 3,000	3
1,001 – 2,000	2
less than 1,000	1

Figure 1

In practice, after eliminating all other races, the backer should give each of the day's surviving races with 10 or fewer runners a rating based on its *class*, as reflected by the *prize money* its winner will collect, i.e. the race's *penalty value* as indicated in newspapers. In fact this class rating, as indicated in the right-hand column in figure 1, is the first figure that should be keyed into the calculator's memory (or simply entered for later augmentation if this facility is not available on the particular machine being used).

An example taken from a prestigious recently contested race – the 1991 Coronation Cup, run at Epsom the day after the Derby – should make what is involved crystal clear.

3.45 *Hanson Coronation Cup (Group 1).*
    Winner £82,542   **1m4f10y**

Since the winner of this race was due to collect £82,542 it received a class rating (based on this prize money) of 17 points as can be seen from the above table.

As is suggested by the frequently voiced belief that in some years Epsom Derby fields are "sub-standard", sizeable prize money alone is no guarantee that races will actually be contested by top-class performers which tend to run up to their best form more often and provide win and place dividends more frequently than do more moderate racehorses. Thus the backer should key in a second numerical assessment into the calculator's memory of the actual ability of those that are due to take part in the race under consideration.

Average of (a) average of Topspeed's three highest ratings and (b) that of Postmark's equivalent figures	Points to be awarded
141 +	18
136 − 140	17
130 − 135	16
124 − 129	15
118 − 123	14
112 − 117	13
106 − 111	12
100 − 105	11
94 − 99	10
88 − 93	9
82 − 87	8
76 − 81	7
70 − 75	6
64 − 69	5
58 − 63	4
52 − 57	3
46 − 51	2
41 − 45	1

Figure 2

In doing this, the backer should enlist the help of two (private) handicappers. These, "Postmark" and "Topspeed" of the *Racing Post*, in assessing horses' form and time performances respectively (and most conveniently) work to the same scales – 0-140, 0-10st for flat racing and 0-175, 0-12st 7lb for jumping races – as the official Jockey Club handicapper and thus both usefully allow their ratings to be directly compared with the official "marks".

All you have to do is work out (a) the average of Postmark's top three ratings for the race and (b) the average of the three highest ratings Topspeed provides and then calculate the average of (a) and (b). The resultant figure for the race is then awarded points according to its size, as is shown in figure 2.

This may sound a little complicated but is actually quite straightforward, as should emerge from the following worked example covering the previously featured (seven runner) Coronation Cup run at Epsom. This was assessed by Postmark and Topspeed as shown in figures 3 and 4.

Jockey Club *Adjusted* Rating	**3.45**		POSTMARK
124 **Karinga Bay**	9-00		130
134 **Quest For Fame**	9-00		140
131 **Rock Hopper**	9-00		139
132 **Sapience**	9-00		136
128 **Spritsail**	9-00		141
133 **Terimon**	9-00		136
137 **In The Groove**	8-11		151◀

Figure 3

HORSE & RATING FROM LAST RUN	3.45	MASTER RATING – DATE, COURSE, DIST, GOING
In The Groove (94)	....	Aug 21 York 10.5gd **129**
Terlmon (120)	....	Jul 28 Asct 12gf **126**
Karinga Bay (80)	....	Jul 31 Gdwd 12gf **122**
Quest For Fame (-)	....	Jun 6 Epsm 12gd **122**
Rock Hopper (83)	....	Apr 20 Newb 12gd **119**
Spritsall (98)	....	Oct 4 Nmkt 12gd **116**
Sapience (90)	....	Jul 28 Asct 12gf **90**

Figure 4

In line with the above table the average of Postmark's top three ratings (i.e. of 151, 141 and 140 = 432 ÷ 3 = 144) was first taken. When applied to Topspeed's top three ratings this same averaging process gave a figure of 126 (i.e. 377 ÷ 3). The average of these two average figures (one for class on form and the other for class on time) worked out at 135 and this, according to figure 2, gave a score of 16 that was next added into the calculator's memory.

Having thus thoroughly rated the class of a qualifying non-handicap according to both the prize money it carries and the calibre of its contestants as rated by private handicappers working on past form and previous performances against the clock, it is time to assess the race according to a third criterion. This involves the *distance* over which it is to be staged for the simple reason that a horse which watch holders and form assessors feel has a sizeable pull over its rivals will be able to make this advantage really tell if it is due to race over a considerable distance of ground.

Thus a rating is next added into the calculator's

'Previous performances against the clock'

memory to reflect the number of furlongs the race under consideration involves. The more furlongs covered, the greater the rating score keyed in, as can be seen in figure 5.

In the case of the race previously featured – the one-and-a-half-mile Coronation Cup – this was credited with a "race distance" score of eight points.

The final and fourth stage of allotting a "suitability for investment" score to a qualifying race involves an assessment of how competitive or otherwise it seems. The latter state is obviously what the backer should seek to capitalize upon and, in general, its possible presence

Distance of race in furlongs	Score to be awarded
22	18
21	17
20	16
19	15
18	14
17	13
16	12
15	11
14	10
13	9
12	8
11	7
10	6
9	5
8	4
7	3
6	2
5	1

Figure 5

'Useable Pull'

will be signalled if the race under consideration can be seen to have attracted a small number of runners.

In the belief that the racing adage "the bigger the field, the bigger the certainty" is illogical, your chosen race is given a score according to figure 6.

Thus the previously featured Coronation Cup, having attracted seven runners, was given a rating of 8 which was the final figure that was added into the memory of the calculator. Interestingly this, as a true punter's "friend", pointed to this top-class Group I

Number of runners	Points to be awarded
2	18
3	16
4	14
5	12
6	10
7	8
8	6
9	4
10	2

Figure 6

all-aged one-and-a-half-mile championship race as being that most suitable for winner finding by calculator on Thursday, 6 June, 1991. This race had, after all, been credited with a high final score of 49 – i.e. 17 (for its prize money) plus 16 (for the class of its highest-rated contenders) plus 8 (for its distance) plus 8 (for its small, seven-runner field).

Those backers who cannot gain access to the specialist racing daily, the *Racing Post*, should add in three of the four figures discussed above into the calculator's memory. These are the first (relating to prize money), the third (relating to race distance) and the fourth (relating to the number of runners due to compete) – all of which are shown in any daily or evening newspaper that has a racing page.

3.45 *Hanson Coronation Cup (Group 1).*
   £110,000 added (£82,542)   **1m4f(7)**

As can be seen above, such a publication would have given sufficient information for the featured Coronation Cup to have been given an "investment suitability" rating of 33 (i.e. 17 for prize money + 8 for race distance + 8 for attracting seven runners).

Points table for flat race selection

Points to be awarded each time a factor is considered	Class Factor 1: prize money to winner (penalty value in £)	Class Factor 2: (a) average of Postmark Ratings for top 3 rated and (b) that of Topspeed	Factor 3: distance of race in furlongs	Factor 4: number of runners
18	100,001 or more	141+	22	2
17	50,000 — 100,000	136 — 140	21	
16	40,001 — 50,000	130 — 135	20	3
15	30,001 — 40,000	124 — 129	19	
14	20,001 — 30,000	118 — 123	18	4
13	15,001 — 20,000	112 — 117	17	
12	12,501 — 15,000	106 — 111	16	5

Figure 7

11	10,001 — 12,500	100 — 105	15	
10	9,001 — 10,000	94 — 99	14	6
9	8,001 — 9,000	88 — 93	13	
8	7,001 — 8,000	82 — 87	12	7
7	6,001 — 7,000	76 — 81	11	
6	5,001 — 6,000	70 — 75	10	8
5	4,001 — 5,000	64 — 69	9	
4	3,001 — 4,000	58 — 63	8	9
3	2,001 — 3,000	52 — 57	7	
2	1,001 — 2,000	46 — 51	6	10
1	less than 1,001	41 — 45	5	

Figure 7 (continued)

Points table for jumping race selection

Points to be awarded each time a factor is considered	Class Factor 1: prize money to winner in £	Class Factor 2: (a) Topspeed's average rating for race and (b) that of Postmark	Class Factor 3: distance of race in furlongs	Class Factor 4: number of runners
18	over 50,000	171+	Over 32	2
17	40,001 – 50,000	161 – 170	32	
16	30,001 – 40,000	151 – 160	31	3
15	20,001 – 30,000	141 – 150	30	
14	15,001 – 20,000	131 – 140	29	4
13	12,501 – 15,000	121 – 130	28	
12	10,001 – 12,500	111 – 120	27	5

Figure 8   28

11	8,501 — 10,000	101 — 110	26	
10	7,001 — 8,500	91 — 100	25	6
9	6,001 — 7,000	81 — 90	24	
8	5,001 — 6,000	71 — 80	23	7
7	4,001 — 5,000	61 — 70	22	
6	3,001 — 4,000	51 — 60	21	8
5	2,501 — 3,000	41 — 50	20	
4	2,001 — 2,500	31 — 40	19	9
3	1,501 — 2,000	21 — 30	18	
2	1,001 — 1,500	11 — 20	17	10
1	less than 1,001	1 — 10	16	

Figure 8 (continued.)   29

Summary

For convenience, the procedures described so far are presented above in the form of a condensed table to facilitate entry into the calculator of the figures required for the crucial initial process of selecting the flat race that is most suitable for investment purposes.

Naturally assessments relating to the suitability for investment purposes of hurdle races and steeplechases can just as readily be made according to the four criteria already described. This will be possible if the second condensed table (page 29) is used. This reflects the fact that races staged under National Hunt rules are generally worth less to their winners than is the case on the Flat, take place over longer distances and feature horses that Postmark and Topspeed assess, not from 1-140 (0-10st) but from 0-175 (0-12st 7lb).

Example Were (implausibly) a jumping race worth over £50,000 to its winner, to involve just two runners whose time and form ratings, as given in the *Racing Post*, averaged out at over 170 and, were it due to be run over in excess of four miles, it would be given an unassailable "investment suitability" rating of $4 \times 18 = 72$.

CHAPTER 2

Calculating what to bet by computing horse race form

Having determined, on the basis of its highest points score – memory —added into your calculator from the tables in Chapter One — which Flat or National Hunt race presents conditions that should both justify and ease the further crucial task of winner-finding, it is time to perform this with your calculator.

The starting point for this crucial process consists of additions of the already discussed ratings of Postmark and Topspeed which are compatible in that they are based on the same scales of 0-140 (0-10st) for flat racing or, for jumping races, of 0-175 (0-12st 7lb).

These combined figures are then averaged by being halved and the resultant figures are the first ones that are entered into the calculator's memory. Hereafter, most reassuringly, this generally under-utilised device really comes into its own as it "forces" the backer to take account of several variables that long experience and also the advice of private handicappers suggest so often exert a crucial influence on the outcomes of many races.

Whatever calculator you use, it will tackle the task of winner-finding in a manner that is far more scientific, comprehensive, objective and relevant than the *modus operandi* of the most disciplined and unemotional of horse players. Such a thought is most encouraging since the ability of 50 such individuals to behave like computers in processing a mass of data in a complex, interactive way recently led two researchers from Cornell University to class their decision-making as comparable to that of brain surgeons.

Understandably, then, my consideration of what variables to take account of in assessing horses' winning prospects has involved what these Cornell researchers identified as the key elements in the thinking of these 50 "super punters". Significantly and most reassuringly, these in fact correspond with many of the "raceday" factors, which some compilers of newspaper private handicaps so regret they have been unable to consider 24 hours before racing that they actually refer to them in caveats they append to their ratings. Of these "raceday" factors, fitness is so crucial that Peter Braddock makes it a cornerstone of the selection method he recommends in his *Complete Guide to Horse Race Selection and Betting* (Longmans, 1987).

Moreover, in one of the best general guides to racing ever published, Kenneth Stewart's *A Background to Racing* (J A Allen, 1978), designations such as "fit to run", "fit to run a good race" and "fit to win" were used to differentiate between runners that, through recent outings on the racecourse, or lack of these, could, or could not, be expected to run up to their previous form.

To take account of the fitness of a runner, a certain

'Super punter'

number of points is added to the average of its combined form and time rating, as indicated in figure 9.

The figures that result from this amendment process are next adjusted to take account of the possible suitability to the contender concerned of the crucial factors which Postmark and Topspeed do not include in their calculations, but which are revealed in the *Racing Post*'s extensive form coverage. This involves further bonus points being added to a runner's rating as indicated in the course, distance and going table (figure 10).

Whatever horse emerges as top-rated after this second, rather sophisticated, amendment of averaged-out amalgamations of "raw" form and time ratings is definitely one for the busy backer who uses a pocket calculator to work on data in the *Racing Post* to consider seriously.

Days since horse last ran on a racecourse*	Number of points to be awarded, ie added to rating
1 — 2	10
3 — 6	9
7 — 10	8
11 — 14	7
15 — 21	6
22 — 28	5
29 — 35	4
36 — 50	3
51 — 100	2
101 +	1

Figure 9 (*This information is usually given in brackets after the names of the runners.)

To make matters really plain the following is a worked example showing exactly what happened when the ratings that Postmark and Topspeed in this

Conditions	Points to be awarded
Runner has gained *more* than one previous win over course and distance *and* has won over prevailing going	8
Runner has gained one previous course and distance win *and* won on prevailing going *or alternatively* has gained a course victory over a different distance, a distance win elsewhere and also won on prevailing going	6
Runner has gained a course win over a different distance *and* has scored on prevailing going *or* won over a different distance on the course and going *or* has gained a course and distance victory on different going	4
Runner has *merely* a course win *or* a distance win on another course *or* a past win over a different distance on the prevailing going	2

Figure 10

newspaper gave to each runner contesting the 1991 Coronation Cup were added, averaged and then adjusted to take account of race fitness and the suitability to the horses concerned of the Epsom course, the 12 furlong race distance and the good-to-firm going that prevailed on the Derby course on Thursday, 6 June, 1991.

For convenience the ratings accorded the Coronation Cup field by Postmark and Topspeed are again shown in figures 11 and 12.

Jockey Club *Adjusted* Rating	**3.45**	POSTMARK
124 **Karinga Bay** 9-00		130
134 **Quest For Fame** 9-00		140
131 **Rock Hopper** 9-00		139
132 **Sapience** 9-00		136
128 **Spritsail** 9-00		141
133 **Terimon** 9-00		136
137 **In The Groove** 8-11		151◄

Figure 11

HORSE & RATING FROM LAST RUN	**3.45**	MASTER RATING – DATE, COURSE, DIST, GOING
In The Groove (94)		Aug 21 York 10.5gd **129**
Terimon (120)		Jul 28 Asct 12gf **126**
Karinga Bay (80)		Jul 31 Gdwd 12gf **122**
Quest For Fame (-)		Jun 6 Epsm 12gd **122**
Rock Hopper (83)		Apr 20 Newb 12gd **119**
Spritsail (98)		Oct 4 Nmkt 12gd **116**
Sapience (90)		Jul 28 Asct 12gf **90**

Figure 12

When combined Postmark's and Topspeed's figures became:

In the Groove	280
Quest for Fame	262
Terimon	262
Rock Hopper	258
Spritsail	257
Karinga Bay	252
Sapience	226

When averaged out (ie divided by two) these ratings changed to:

In the Groove	140
Quest for Fame	131
Terimon	131
Rock Hopper	129
Spiritsail	128
Karinga Bay	126
Sapience	113

The above ratings formed the starting point for calculations involving each runner for the Coronation Cup of 1991 and, as such, were entered into the calculator's memory.

Next the fitness points table (see figure 9, *page 34*) was consulted and further points keyed in for each runner, to reflect its race fitness or lack of this (see figure 13, *page 39*). This changed the runners' ratings to:

In the Groove	$140 + 6 = 146$
Terimon	$131 + 3 = 134$
Spritsail	$128 + 6 = 134$
Rock Hopper	$129 + 4 = 133$
Quest for Fame	$131 + 1 = 132$
Karinga Bay	$126 + 4 = 130$
Sapience	$113 + 1 = 114$

Next the course, distance and going table (see figure 10, *page 35*) was consulted. To allow this to take account of the last-mentioned of these three factors –the good-to-firm ground that prevailed at Epsom on 6 June, 1991 – the runners' form summaries as given in the *Racing Post* were consulted (see figure 14, *page 40*).

After points from the course distance and going table (figure 10) had, where appropriate, been memory-added to each runner's score, the following figures appeared on the calculator's display panel:

In the Groove	148 (i.e. 146 + 2)
Spritsail	138 (i.e. 134 + 4)
Rock Hopper	137 (i.e. 133 + 4)
Quest for Fame	136 (i.e. 132 + 4)
Terimon	136 (i.e. 134 + 2)
Karinga Bay	134 (i.e. 130 + 4)
Sapience	120 (i.e. 114 + 6)

Thus In the Groove finally emerged, with a rating of 148, as superior by the equivalent of 10lbs to his nearest rival and, gratifyingly, this classy four-year-old won readily at the most acceptable odds of 7-2.

Next an even more advanced method of horse race selection by calculator will be described and, as is only to be expected, this again involves data provided in a specialist racing daily – this time, however, in the *Sporting Life*.

As class is such a crucial factor, it again plays a prominent part in calculations but, on this occasion, it is assessed by dividing the amount that a horse has won in its racing lifetime by the number of victories it has registered in this time. If, for example, the first

Figure 13

3.45 *Hanson Coronation Cup (Group 1).* **1m4f10y** [CH4]
Winner £82,542

£110,000 added For four yrs old and upwards Weights Colts and geldings.9st; fillies 8st 11lb Entries 25 pay £580 Forfeit 19 pay £660
Confirmed 8 pay £410 Penalty Value 1st £82,542 2nd £30,624 3rd £14,487 4th £6,068 POSTMARK

| 1 (3) | 5136-33 | **KARINGA BAY**³⁴ [D] | Denys Smith | 4 9-00 | B Rouse | (139) |

K Higson *royal blue, white cross of lorraine, red cap, white spots.*

| 2 (6) | 2/1215- | **QUEST FOR FAME**³⁴⁰ [CDBF] | R Charlton | 4 9-00 | Pat Eddery | (140) |

K Abdullah *green, pink sash and cap, white sleeves.*

| 3 (7) | 1/21-11 | **ROCK HOPPER**³⁴ [D] | M R Stoute | 4 9-00 | W Carson | (139) |

Maktoum Al Maktoum *royal blue, white chevron, light blue cap.*

| 4 (1) | 6/2219- | **SAPIENCE**³¹³ [CD] | J G FitzGerald | 5 9-00 | W R Swinburn | (136) |

W H O'Gorman *yellow, dark blue hoops, yellow sleeves and cap.*

| 5 (2) | 3/313-1 | **SPRITSAIL**¹⁶ [D] | H R A Cecil | 5 9-00 | L Piggott | (141) |

Lady Howard de Walden *apricot, black sash and cap.*

| 6 (4) | 32640-1 | **TERIMON**⁵⁰ | C E Brittain | 5 9-00 | M Roberts | (136) |

The Dowager Lady Beaverbrook *beaver brown, maple leaf green cross-belts and cap.*

| 7 (5) | 1391-12 | **IN THE GROOVE**²⁶ [BF] | D R C Elsworth | 4 8-11 | S Cauthen | (151) |

Brian Cooper *grey and maroon (halved), sleeves reversed, grey and maroon quartered cap.*

LAST YEAR: **IN THE WINGS** A Fabre, France 4 9 00 C Asmussen

BETTING FORECAST: 7-4 Rock Hopper, 9-4 In The Groove, 9-2 Quest For Fame, 5 Spritsail, 10 Terimon, 33 Karinga Bay

39

3.45

Hanson Coronation Cup
1m 4f 10y – 7 declared
4yo+ Gp1 – £82,542

In The Groove

b f Night Shift – Pine Ridge (High Top)
Placings: 2213/281141391-12
D R C Elsworth 4 8-11

	Starts	1st	2nd	3rd	Win & Pl
	15	6	4	2	£676,900

4/91 Sand	1m Gp2 good	£37,818
10/90 Nmkt	1m2f Gp1 good	£255,100
8/90 York	1m2f110y Gp1 good	£180,338
5/90 Curr	1m 3yo Gp1 good	£119,625
5/90 York	1m2f110y 3yo Gp3 gd-fm	£23,679
8/89 York	6f Mdn 2yo gd-fm	£7,505
	Total win prizemoney	£624,065

17 May Newbury 1m   Gp2 £40.902
4 ran   GD-SFT   Time 1m42.70s (slw4.0s)

1 Polar Falcon 4 9-0 .... L Piggott ²3/1
2 **IN THE GROOVE** 4 9-2 .... S Cauthen ³1/2F
*held up, ridden and led over 1f out, headed
inside final furlong, unable to quicken*
          [op 1/3]
3 Candy Glen 4 9-5 .... E Maple ⁴7/1
Dist: 2-¾-4   Postmark: 124/120/122

26 Apr Sandown 1m   Gp2 £37,818
5 ran   GOOD   Time 1m42.45s (slw1.4s)

1 **IN THE GROOVE** 4 9-3 .... S Cauthen ⁵15/8
*5th straight, headway 2f out, led inside final
furlong, ran on well* [op 5/4 tchd 2/1 in plcs]
2 Zoman 4 9-4 .... T Quinn ⁴7/4F
3 Aldbourne 5 8-11 .... L Piggott ¹13/1
Dist: 1-2½-2½-12   Postmark: 131/130/118

20 Oct90 Newmarket 1m2f   Gp1 £255,100
10 ran   GOOD   Time 2m05.67s (slw0.5s)

Quest For Fame

*b c Rainbow Quest – Aryenne
(Green Dancer)*
Placings: 2/1215-
R Charlton 4 9-0

	Starts	1st	2nd	3rd	Win & Pl
	5	2	2	–	£385.366

6/90 Epsm	1m4f 3yo Gp1 good	£355.000
4/90 Newb	1m3f Mdn 3yo good	£4.272
	Total win prizemoney	£359.272

1 Jul90 The Curragh 1m4f   3yo Gp1 £309.500
9 ran   YIELD   Time 2m33.0s

1 Salsabil 3 8-11 .... W Carson ⁹11/4
2 Deploy 3 9-0 .... W R Swinburn ⁷16/1
3 Belmez 3 9-0 .... S Cauthen ¹4/1
5 **QUEST FOR FAME** 3 9-0 .. Pat Eddery ⁸5/4F
Dist: ¾-4-½-nk-2½
Postmark: 129/128/122/121/121

6 Jun90 Epsom 1m4f   3yo Gp1 £355.000
18 ran   GOOD   Time 2m37.26s (slw1.4s)

1 **QUEST FOR FAME** 3 9-0 ... Pat Eddery ¹⁰7/1
*2nd straight, led well over 1f out, ran on
well*   [op 8/1]

1 **IN THE GROOVE** 3 8-9 .... S Cauthen ²9/2
*held up, headway 2f out, led over 1f out,
driven out*   [op 4/1 tchd 5/1]
2 Linamix 3 8-12 .... F Head ³14/1
3 Legal Case 4 9-3 .... L Dettori ⁵6/1
10 **TERIMON** 4 9-3 .... Pat Eddery ⁷12/1
*held up, effort over 3f out, no impression,
btn 41 lengths*   [op 12/1 tchd 14/1]
Dist: 1½-¾-3½-5-hd   Postmark: 128/127/†26

21 Aug90 York 1m2f110y   Gp1 £180,338
9 ran   GOOD   Time 2m08.77s (fst1.4s)

1 **IN THE GROOVE** 3 8-9 .... S Cauthen ³4/1
*held up and behind, quickened to lead well
over 1f out, ran on well*
         [op 3/1 tchd 9/2 in odd plcs]
2 Elmaamul 3 8-12 .... W Carson ¹7/2
3 Batshoof 4 9-6 .... Pat Eddery ⁵5/2F
4 **TERIMON** 4 9-6 .... M Roberts ⁴11/1
*held up, not clear run 3f out. ran on
approaching final furlong* [op 7/1 tchd 12/1]
Dist: 1½-2½-½-¾-5 Postmark: 127/127/122/121

Figure 14

40

2 Blue Stag 3 9-0 .... C Asmussen [13]8/1
3 Elmaamul 3 9-0 .... W Carson [4]10/1
5 KARINGA BAY 3 9-0 .... B Rouse [5]14/1
8th straight, no headway final 2f [op 12/1]
Dist: 3-1½-2½-2-hd
Postmark: 126/121/119/116/114

8 May90 Chester 1m4f65y 3yo Gp3 £24,771
3 ran GOOD Time 2m41.42s (slw4.6s)

1 Belmez 3 8-11 .... S Cauthen [1]8/13F
2 **QUEST FOR FAME** 3 8-11 Pat Eddery [3]10/3
held up, quickened to challenge 5f out, led entering straight, headed 1f out, kept on [op 3/1 tchd 7/2]
3 Missionary Ridge 3 8-11 ...... W Carson [2]4/1
Dist: 1-10 Postmark: 117/114/102

Rock Hopper

b c Shareef Dancer – Cormorant Wood (Home Guard)
Placings: 511/21-11
M R Stoute **4 9-0**

	Starts	1st	2nd	3rd	Win & Pl
	7	5	1	–	£123,876
5/91 Nmkt 1m4f Gp2 good					£39,186
4/91 Newb 1m4f Gp3 good					£24,813
5/90 Ling 1m3f106y 3yo Gp3 gd-fm					£35,230
11/89 Nmkt 1m2f 2yo List gd-sft					£11,063
10/89 Nott 1m2f Mdn 2yo gd-fm					£1,920
			Total win prizemoney £112,212		

3 May Newmarket 1m4f Gp2 £39,186
8 ran GOOD Time 2m34.48s (slw2.9s)

1 **ROCK HOPPER** 4 8-7 ...... Pat Eddery [6]8/11F
held up, not clear run 2f out, switched over 1f out, quickened to lead inside final furlong, soon clear and eased, pushed out close home [op 4/5 tchd 1/1]
2 Mountain Kingdom 7 8-10 . S Cauthen [2]25/1
3 **KARINGA BAY** 4 8-7 .... B Rouse [8]13/2
tracked leaders, challenged 3f out, slight lead over 1f out, headed inside final furlong, kept on [op 6/1 tchd 7/1]
Dist: nk-1½-2½-2-1 Postmark: 119/121/116

20 Apr Newbury 1m4f Gp3 £24,813
10 ran GOOD Time 2m32.9s

---

1 **ROCK HOPPER** 4 8-10 ..... Pat Eddery [10]3/1F
headway 3f out, led inside final furlong, pushed out [op 3/1 tchd 7/2 & 11/4]
2 Warm Fooling 4 8-10 .... M Hills [19]9/2
3 Rudjig 5 8-11 .... S Cauthen [5]12/1
Dist: ¾-hd-6-10 Postmark: 125/122/108

12 May90 Lingfield 1m3f106y
3yo Gp3 £35,230
5 ran GD-FM Time 2m28.35s (slw2.5s)

1 **ROCK HOPPER** 3 9-0 ..... W R Swinburn [1]9/4
3rd straight, led over 2f out, ridden out [op 5/2 tchd 11/4,
3/1 in a place & 85/40 in a place]
2 Benzine 3 9-0 .... T Quinn [4]14/1
3 Great Heights 3 9-0 .... S Cauthen [5]3/1
Dist: 2-4-4-3 Postmark: 107/102/97

Terimon

gr h Bustino – Nicholas Grey (Track Spare)
Placings: 82462231224/1632640-1
C E Brittain **5 9-0**

	Starts	1st	2nd	3rd	Win & Pl
	19	3	6	2	£271,080
4/91 Nmkt 1m1f Gp3 gd-fm					£22,221
4/90 Nmkt 1m1f Gp3 gd-fm					£22,032
5/89 Leic 1m2f Mdn 3yo gd-fm					£1,884
			Total win prizemoney £46,137		

17 Apr Newmarket 1m1f Gp3 £22,221
11 ran GD-FM Time 1m49.23s (fst2.8s)

1 **TERIMON** 5 8-13 .... M Roberts [8]7/2F
held up, effort 2f out, ran on well to lead well inside final furlong [op 3/1 tchd 4/1]
2 Emperor Fountain 4 8-10 ... W Newnes [4]14/1
3 Ruby Tiger 4 8-12 .... T Quinn [9]9/1
Dist: nk-nk-nk-1-shd Postmark: 119/115/116

20 Oct90 Newmarket 1m2f Gp1 £255,100
tenth, see **IN THE GROOVE**

21 Aug90 York 1m2f110y Gp1 £180,338
fourth, see **IN THE GROOVE**

28 Jul90 Ascot 1m4f Gp1 £284,715
11 ran GD-FM Time 2m30.76s (fst1.6s)

1 Belmez 3 8-9 .... M J Kinane [11]15/2
2 Old Vic 4 9-7 .... S Cauthen [1]4/1

Figure 14 (continued)

41

3 Assatis 5 9-7 .... M Shibata [9] 16/1
6 **TERIMON** 4 9-7 .... M Roberts [7] 15/2
8th straight, never near to challenge
                        [op 8/1 tchd 9/1 & 7/1]
9 **SAPIENCE** 4 9-7 .... Pat Eddery [5] 8/1
prominent until weakened and 6th straight,
eased when beaten over 2f out, btn
34 lengths   [op 7/1 tchd 9/1]
Dist: nk-1½-5-1-1½
Postmark: 132/131/128/122/121/120

Sapience

ch h Niniski – Claretta (Roberto)
Placings: 4110281226/2219-
J G FitzGerald   **5 9-0**

	Starts	1st	2nd	3rd	Win & Pl
	14	4	5	–	£216,992
Ⓡ 88	7/90 Nmkt	1m4f Gp2 good..................			£48,138
	8/89 York	1m6f (0–115) Hcp gd-fm			£69,370
	8/88 Epsm	1m110y 2yo Grad-fm			£3,909
	8/88 Ches	7f Mdn 2yo good			£2,385
				Total win prizemoney	£123,802

28 Jul90 Ascot 1m4f   Gp1 £284,715
ninth, see **TERIMON**

10 Jul90 Newmarket 1m4f   Gp2 £48,138
7 ran   GOOD   Time 2m34.96s (slw3.9s)

1 **SAPIENCE** 4 9-0 .... Pat Eddery [4] 11/2
made all, stayed on strongly final furlong
                                        [op 5/1]
2 Charmer 5 9-0 .... M Roberts [7] 20/1
3 Assatis 5 9-5.................... R Cochrane [6] 13/2
Dist: ¾-2½-1½-hd-shd   Postmark: 122/120/121

17 May90 York 1m6f   Gp2 £47,223
6 ran   GOOD   Time 2m56.79s (slw0.2s)

1 Braashee 4 8-9 .... M Roberts [3] 11/8F
2 **SAPIENCE** 4 8-9 .... Pat Eddery [4] 3/1
3rd straight, challenged on bit over 2f out,
soon led, headed 2f out, ridden and not
quicken inside final furlong   [op 5/2]
3 Top Class 5 8-12 .... B Marcus [5] 12/1
Dist: ¾-4-3-2½-20   Postmark: 115/114/112

Karinga Bay

ch c Ardross – Handy Dancer (Green God)
Placings: 6117/325136-33
Denys Smith   **4 9-0**

	Starts	1st	2nd	3rd	Win & Pl
	12	3	1	4	£100,067
	7/90 Gdwd	1m4f 3yo Gp3 gd-fm...........			£30,024
	8/89 Newb	7f 2yo List good			£10,283
	7/89 York	6f Mdn 2yo gd-fm.................			£3,785
				Total win prizemoney	£44,092

3 May Newmarket 1m4f   Gp2 £39,186
third, see **ROCK HOPPER**

27 Apr Sandown 1m2f   Gp3 £23,550
6 ran   GOOD   Time 2m07.23s (slw0.7s)

1 Noble Patriarch 4 8-10 .... J Reid [4] 7/1
2 Stapleford Manor 4 8-10 .... L Dettori [6] 2/1F
3 **KARINGA BAY** 4 8-13 .... B Rouse [3] 10/3
3rd straight, led over 2f out until 1f out, one
pace   [op 7/2 tchd 4/1 & 3/1]
Dist: 3-¾-1½-1½-7   Postmark: 118/112/114

15 Sep90 Doncaster 1m6f127y

                              3yo Gp1 £151,939
8 ran   GOOD   Time 3m08.78s (fst0.5s)

1 Snurge 3 9-0 .... T Quinn [8] 7/2
2 Hellenic 3 8-11 .... W R Swinburn [1] 2/1F

3 River God 3 9-0 .... S Cauthen [3] 10/3
6 **KARINGA BAY** 3 9-0 .... B Rouse [4] 11/1
chased leaders, effort and chance over 4f
out, ridden and beaten 3f out
                          [op 10/1 tchd 12/1 in plcs]
Dist: ¾-4-3-½-1
Postmark: 126/122/120/117/117/116

6 Jun90 Epsom 1m4f   3yo Gp1 £355,000
fifth, see **QUEST FOR FAME**

Spritsail

b h Kalaglow – Set Sail (Alpenkonig)
Placings: 111311413/313-1
H R A Cecil   **5 9-0**

Figure 14 (continued)

42

	Starts	1st	2nd	3rd	Win & Pl
	13	8	–	4	£79,344
5/91 Gdwd 1m2f List gd-fm					£14,100
10/90 Nmkt 1m4f List good					£11,648
10/89 Nmkt 1m4f List gd-fm					£10,868
7/89 Chep 1m4f gd-fm					£10,770
6/89 Asct 1m4f 3yo firm					£7,684
5/89 Ling 1m4f 3yo firm					£2,924
4/89 Ripn 1m1f Grad soft					£1,814
10/88 Rdcr 7f Mdn 2yo good					£3,890
Total win prizemoney					£63,698

21 May Goodwood 1m2f   List £14,100
6 ran   GD-FM   Time 2m07.64s (slw1.5s)
1 **SPRITSAIL** 5 9-1 .... Pat Eddery ²9/4
3rd straight. led 2f out. ridden out
              [op 5/2 tchd 11/4. 3/1 in a place]
2 Lord Charmer 4 8-12 .... W Carson ⁴13/8F
3 Game Plan 4 9-2 .... M Roberts ¹9/2
Dist: 2½-5-6-10-2   Postmark: 127/117/111

27 Oct90 Newbury 1m4f   Gp3 £21,465
8 ran   SOFT   Time 2m44.79s (slw11.9s)
1 Down The Flag 3 8-7 .... B Raymond ⁹5/1
2 Hajade 3 8-7 .... J Fortune ⁵13/2
3 **SPRITSAIL** 4 9-0 .... W Ryan ⁶5/2
3rd straight. every chance over 2f out. hard ridden. one pace   [op 6/4]
Dist: 1½-7-1½-5-8   Postmark: 117/114/106

4 Oct90 Newmarket 1m4f   List £11,648
11 ran   GOOD   Time 2m27.55s (fst4.1s)
1 **SPRITSAIL** 4 9-3 .... S Cauthen ³13/8F
held up. led over 1f out. comfortably
           [op 7/4 tchd 2/1 (9/4 in plcs)]
2 Ahead 3 7-12 .... G Carter ⁶13/2
3 Per Quod 5 9-3 .... B Raymond ²13/2
Dist: 2½-1-7-2½-1½   Postmark: 121/104/114

Figure 14 (continued)

Sporting Life figure indicating such prize money (not the
bracketed second figure which, where applicable,
relates to winning sums gained in the current season
only) was £9,987, as in the example in figure 15, and
the number of individual victories the horse has
gained in its career (which can be gleaned from the
details of these shown in its form summary) was seen
to be two, a simple process of division would reveal
that its average "pick-up" as a past winner has been
£4,993.

The backer should delete the last two digits of this
average prize-money figure (and round up or down
what remains), as in the above example, where the
figure in question (from £4,993) would be 50. This
figure should be keyed into your calculator prior to
pressing its + key.

Next, all of the entries appearing in a horse's
formline should be accorded points according to

2311P3-433 ONLY TROUBLE (9-11-8) (T J
Houlbrooke) b or br m Trasi's Son - Kadella by
Kadir Cup **1988-89, 2½m ch heavy (Haydock),
3m ch heavy (Chepstow). £9,987 (-).**
  LWR (89+90): 2m4f ch 96 (Dis)   TR: **106**

  Jan 8, Wolverhampton, 3m 1f h'cap chase
(0-135), good, £3,054: 1 Rymer King (8-10-11),
2 A Boy Named Sioux (10-10-4), 3 ONLY
TROUBLE (9-10-5, H Davies), **always prominent, led tenth till headed 15th, ridden two
out, kept on one pace.** (5 to 1 op 7 to 1 tchd 8
to 1); 9 Ran. 1l, 8l, 3l, 20l, 5l. 6m 23.60s (a
8.60s).
RACECHECK: Wins 0, pl 2, unpl 4.

  Dec 23, Chepstow, 2½m h'cap chase
(0-125), soft, £3,039: 1 The Leggett (6-10-7), 2
Wally Wombat (11-10-1), 3 ONLY TROUBLE
(8-10-11, B Powell), **chased leaders until lost
place halfway, stayed on again from two
out.** (4 to 1 op 5 to 1 tchd 6 to 1); 13 Ran. 12l, 7l,
4l, 3l, 6l. 5m 16.50s (a 26.50s). SR: 24/6/9/-/-/1.
RACECHECK: Wins 5, pl 6, unpl 13.

  Dec 4, Worcester, 2½m h'cap chase (0-125),
good to firm, £3,392: 1 Toby Tobias (7-12-0), 2
Arctic Cavalier (7-10-7), 3 Pride Hill (7-10-2,5*),
4 ONLY TROUBLE (8-10-10, H Davies),
**pressed leader until weakened approaching
12th.** (11 to 1 op 10 to 1 tchd 12 to 1); 11 Ran. 8l,
2l, 25l, 5l, 8l, sht-hd, 25l. 5m 17.10s (a 21.10s).
RACECHECK: Wins 3, pl 9, unpl 15.

Figure 15

where each of these reveals this animal finished in a
recent contest.

> 10 points should be given for each current
> season win.
> 8 points should be given for each current
> season second.
> 6 points should be given for each current
> season third.
> 4 points should be given for each current
> season fourth.

2 points should be given for each current season fifth.

0 points should be given for each current season place worse than fifth (shown in the *Sporting Life*'s form summary as a "duck's egg").

N.B. If a horse's current season formline consists of more than two entries it is not necessary to take account of any of its previous seasons' form figures that may be included in its formline. If this involves only one or two runs in the current season or no outings at all in this season, calculations should be based on a horse's last three outings irrespective of season.

N.B. If the backer sees the symbols P,R,B or F (which indicate that a runner has been pulled up, has refused to jump a fence, been brought down or has fallen) he should regard such outcomes as "unplaced" runs.

Thus, if a runner's current season formline reads as 433, as in the case of Only Trouble, it would receive a seasonal finishing position score of 16 (see figure 15). This score should be divided by its total number of outings – three. The resultant figure (rounded up or down where necessary) should be keyed into the calculator, prior to pressing its −key. In the above example the figure so entered was 5.33, i.e. 5.

The third factor you should take account of is the horse's position last time out and this means that a previous winner should be given a score of 1, a second last time out 2, a third 3, a fourth 4 and so on. Conveniently, the last right-hand entry in each runner's formline will show the figure required which should be noted as the third to be entered into your calculator, before, on this occasion, pressing the = key and then the × key.

In Only Trouble's case the figure 3 indicated its position last time out and this was keyed in, the = key pressed and the × button depressed.

Finally, comes a sophisticated set of computations that allow full statistical advantage to be taken of a feature only introduced into the *Sporting Life*'s form coverage as recently as the spring of 1990. This is "Racecheck" which indicates how many winners

2311P3-433 ONLY TROUBLE (9-11-8) (T J Houlbrooke) b or br m Trasi's Son - Kadella by Kadir Cup **1988-89, 2½m ch heavy (Haydock), 3m ch heavy (Chepstow). £9,987 (-).**
LWR (89+90): 2m4f ch **96** (Dis)   TR: **106**

Jan 8, Wolverhampton, 3m 1f h'cap chase (0-135), good, £3,054: 1 Rymer King (8-10-11), 2 A Boy Named Sioux (10-10-4), 3 ONLY TROUBLE (9-10-5, H Davies), **always prominent, led tenth till headed 15th, ridden two out, kept on one pace.** (5 to 1 op 7 to 1 tchd 8 to 1); 9 Ran. 1l, 8l, 3l, 20l, 5l. 6m 23.60s (a 8.60s).
RACECHECK: Wins 0, pl 2, unpl 4.

Dec 23, Chepstow, 2½m h'cap chase (0-125), soft, £3,039: 1 The Leggett (6-10-7), 2 Wally Wombat (11-10-1), 3 ONLY TROUBLE (8-10-11, B Powell), **chased leaders until lost place halfway, stayed on again from two out.** (4 to 1 op 5 to 1 tchd 6 to 1); 13 Ran. 12l, 7l, 4l, 3l, 6l. 5m 16.50s (a 26.50s). SR: 24/6/9/-/-/1.
RACECHECK: Wins 5, pl 6, unpl 13.

Dec 4, Worcester, 2½m h'cap chase (0-125), good to firm, £3,392: 1 Toby Tobias (7-12-0), 2 Arctic Cavalier (7-10-7), 3 Pride Hill (7-10-2,5*), 4 ONLY TROUBLE (8-10-10, H Davies), **pressed leader until weakened approaching 12th.** (11 to 1 op 10 to 1 tchd 12 to 1); 11 Ran. 8l, 2l, 25l, 5l, 8l, sht-hd, 25l. 5m 17.10s (a 21.10s).
RACECHECK: Wins 3, pl 9, unpl 15.

Figure 16

(WINS), placed horses (PL) and unplaced horses (UNPL) have come out of a particular race since it was run (see figure 16).

The example of this "Racecheck" feature reveals that on two recent occasions the mare Only Trouble was crucially placed in races whose "productivity" as regards subsequent winners, placed horses and unplaced ones has already been calculated by the *Sporting Life*.

What the backer should do is first discount any "Racecheck" races (like Only Trouble's on 4 December) in which a placing in the first three was not achieved and then compute the "productivity" of all of its other recent races in which it did "make the frame". Here, the grand total of all wins and places shown in the appropriate "Racecheck" entries should first be entered into your calculator before pressing its = key.

In Only Trouble's case, her races on 23 December (in which she came third) and on 8 January (in which she again did so) between them produced 13 as the first figure needed to assess the worth of this runner's recent form (i.e. 5 wins, 6 pl, plus 0 wins, 2 pl) and 30 (i.e. $[5 + 6 + 13] + [0 + 2 + 4]$) as the second. Thus, 13 was entered and the calculator's = key pressed. Then its × key was operated, the number 100 keyed in, the ÷ key engaged and 30 entered, before the = key was pressed and the $\sqrt{}$ key finally engaged. This gave a final rating of 47.47.

Since what was needed to arrive at this may sound rather bewildering and complicated, figure 17 simplifies and summarises what is required in step-by-step format and applies it to Only Trouble's past form.

Step 1 **(Rating prize money)**	Enter first two digits of "average prize money" figure (50 for Only Trouble)
Step 2 **(Rating the formline)**	Press + key Enter formline rating figure (5 for Only Trouble)
Step 3 **(Rating the latest run)**	Press − key Enter last figure shown in current season's formline (3 for Only Trouble) Press = key
Step 4 **(First stage of rating "worth" of recent placed form)**	Press × key Enter "Racecheck" places figure (13 for Only Trouble) Press = key
Step 5 **(Second stage of rating worth of recent placed form)**	Press × key Enter 100 Enter ÷ key Enter Racecheck "total runs" figure (30 for Only Trouble)
Step 6 **(Arriving at a final rating)**	Press = key Press √ key for horse's final rating (for Only Trouble = 47.47)

Figure 17

	A Prize money rating	B Form figure rating	C Position last time out	D "Racecheck" places	E "Racecheck" runs
Astre Radieux	25 (£251ϐ)	6 (62÷10=6)	1 (1st)	11 (2+4+2+3)	25 (2+4+11+2+3+3)
Famous Lad	22	6	2	4	16
Hotplate	24	5	7	1	8
Lough Road	—	3	2	2	5
Romany King	23	6	2	17	40
The Humble Tiller	21	7	1	3	19
Tartan Tempest	15	4	2	1	8

Figure 18a

THE HUMBLE TILLER   **7-10-13**
60/1F3222-41   **N J Henderson**
b g Rarity - Bardicate by Bargello **1988-89 2½m h good/soft (Southwell)**
1989-90 (Mar) 2m 5f ch good (Windsor) nov. **£4,174 (£2,836).**

LWR (89+90): -   TR: **96**

    March 5, Windsor, 2m 5f nov chase, good, £2,836: 1 THE HUMBLE TILLER (7-11-2, R Dunwoody), **chased leaders, led approaching four out, stayed on under pressure run-in.** (9/4 fav op 2/1 tchd 11/4) 2 Bizage Motors (6-11-2), 3 Granny Pray On (8-10-6,5*),; 18 Ran. 2l, 1l, 12l, 4l, 1½l, hd, 10l, 4l. 5m 22.00s (a 5.00s). SR: 7/5/-/-/-/-.
RACECHECK: Wins 2, pl 1, unpl 16.

    Dec 21, Towcester, 2m 5f 110y nov chase, good, £2,210: 1 Castle Oaks (6-11-0), 2 Rambling Echo (8-11-0), 3 Another Striplight (6-10-7,7*), 4 THE HUMBLE TILLER (6-11-0, R Dunwoody), **pressed leaders till weakened after three out.** (7/2 fav op 7/4); 11 Ran. 7l, 8l, 7l, 8l. 5m 48.80s (a 18.80s).

    April 27 1989, Towcester, 2m 5f 26y nov hdle, heavy, £1,088: 1 Market Forces (6-11-11), 2 THE HUMBLE TILLER (6-11-0, J Railton,4*), **progress fifth, every chance two out, not quicken approaching last.** (11/8 fav op 5/4 tchd 6/4) 3 Idiot's Beauty (8-10-13),; 17 Ran. 7l, 20l, 25l, 3l, dist. 5m 59.40s (a 52.40s).

FAMOUS LAD   **7-11-5**
6003/453-B12   **R Lee**
b g Bold Lad - Famous Band by Banderilla
1989-90 (Feb) 2m ch good/soft (Catterick) nov. **£2,228.**

LWR (89+90): -   TR: **102**

    March 3, Hereford, 2m nov chase, soft, £2,721: 1 New Halen (9-11-7,7*), 2 FAMOUS LAD (7-11-6, R Bellamy,5*), **always going well, smooth headway to lead two out, blundered and pecked last, not recover.** (2/1 fav op 5/2) 3 Roman Dart (6-11-11),; 13 Ran. 2½l, 12l, 3l, dist. 4m 9.90s (a 14.90s). SR: 23/17/5/-/-/-.
RACECHECK: Wins 1, pl 3, unpl 12.

    Feb 21, Catterick, 2m nov chase, good to soft, £2,228: 1 FAMOUS LAD (7-11-2, B Dowling), **settled midfield, improved from three out to lead between last two, ran on well.** (20/1 op 16/1) 2 Mr Therm (5-10-4,3*), 3 Beau Guest (8-11-2,7*),; 11 Ran. 3l, sht-hd, 5l, ½l, 4l. 4m 3.50s (a 12.50s).

    Jan 23, Chepstow, 2½m nov chase, heavy, £3,195: 1 Elvercone (9-11-3,v), 2 Celtic Walk (6-11-9), 3 Regal Castle (7-11-3,bl), B FAMOUS LAD (7-11-3, B Dowling), **brought down first.** (33/1 op 25/1); 15 Ran. 12l, 1½l, 10l, 20l, ½l. 5m 32.00s (a 42.00s). SR: 9/3/-/-/-/-.

HOTPLATE   **7-11-10●**
4330121052/142-1F5131P   **D McCain**
ch g Buckskin (FR) - Pencil Lady by Bargello **1987-88 2½m h soft (Newcastle); 2m 1f 110y h heavy (Carlisle) 1988-89 2½m h good/soft (Carlisle)**
1989-90 (Nov) 2m ch good (Haydock) nov; **(Feb) 2m ch good (Carlisle)** Hcp [0-125,120,**96**]; **(Mar) 2m ch soft (Carlisle)** Hcp [Open,130,**103**]. **£14,587 (£10,004).**

LWR (89+90): **103** (5l)   TR: **107**

    April 5, Liverpool, 3m 1f nov chase, good to firm, £21,036: 1 Royal Athlete (7-11-9), 2 Arctic Call (7-11-3,bl), 3 Cahervillahow (6-11-6), P HOTPLATE (7-11-3, M Dwyer), **soon outpaced, behind when pulled up before three out.** (50/1 op 33/1); 11 Ran. ½l, 10l, 15l, nk, 15l. 6m 11.30s (eq ave).
RACECHECK: Wins 0, pl 2, unpl 0.

    March 9, Carlisle, 2m Hcp chase [Open,130], soft, £2,684: 1 HOTPLATE (7-10-4, inc 4lb ow, **103**, M Dwyer), **always going well, led after three out, ran on strongly.** (10/11 op 11/10) 2 Reiver's Lad (9-10-1), 3 Masnoon (7-12-3),; 5 Ran. 5l, 3l, 2l, 20l. 4m 21.90s (a 20.90s).
RACECHECK: Wins 0, pl 1, unpl 7.

    Feb 20, Sedgefield, 2½m Hcp chase [0-125,118], good to soft, £2,476: 1 Sword Beach (6-10-2), 2 Captain Mor (8-10-6), 3 HOTPLATE (7-10-5, **99**, P Niven), **always well placed, every chance and ridden from last, one pace.** (3/1 tchd 7/2); 7 Ran. Nk, 25l, 15l, 15l. 5m 28.20s (a 20.20s). SR: 22/25/20/11/-/-.

LOUGH ROAD   **8-10-12**
252S/000205-P20F2   **Mrs G E Jones**
ch g Laurence O - Vixen's Red by Bargello

LWR (89+90): -   TR: **95**

    April 4, Huntingdon, 3m chase, good to firm, £2,247: 1 Erostin Floats (6-11-7), 2 LOUGH ROAD (8-11-0, J Bryan), **chased leaders, led briefly three out, kept on one pace from next.** (7/2 op 4/1 tchd 9/2) 3 Short List (7-11-0),; 9 Ran. 2l, 7l, 1½l, 30l. 6m 19.20s (a 30.20s).
RACECHECK: Wins 0, pl 1, unpl 3.

    March 21, Worcester, 3m nov chase, good, £4,050: 1 Rambling Echo (9-11-10), 2 Croix de Guerre (9-11-10,bl), 3 Coruscate (8-11-10), F LOUGH ROAD (8-11-10, J Bryan), **always prominent, ridden 14th, challenging in third place when fell two out.** (7/1 op 6/1); 15 Ran. Nk, 12l, 10l, 15l, dist. 5m 59.40s (a 13.40s). SR: 22/21/9/-/-/-.
RACECHECK: Wins 0, pl 5, unpl 9.

Figure 18b

ASTRE RADIEUX (FR)　　　　　　　5-10-12
/4423-4450221221　　　　　　　　　　**S Mellor**
b g Gay Mecene (USA) - Divine Etoile (USA) by
Nijinsky (CAN)
　　1989-90 (Jan) 2½m ch good/soft **(Warwick)**
nov; **(Mar)** 2m ch good **(Hexham)** nov. **£5,033.**

LWR (89+90): -　　　　　　　　　　　TR: **95**

　　March 15, Hexham, 2m nov chase, good,
£2,247: 1 ASTRE RADIEUX (5-11-3, Mr D
Gray), **jumped boldly, made most, clear after
three out, readily.** (4/6 op 8/11) 2 Contact
Kelvin (8-11-4), 3 Majestic Ring (8-11-4),: 13
Ran. 5l, 25l, 3l, 15l, 2l, sht-hd. 4m 5.30s (a
7.30s). SR: 24/20/-/-/-/-.
RACECHECK: Wins 2, pl 4, unpl 11.

　　March 10, Chepstow. See ROMANY KING
　　March 2, Haydock, 2m Hcp chase
[0-125,119], heavy, £3,542: 1 The Leggett
(7-11-11, inc 4lb ex), 2 ASTRE RADIEUX
(5-10-0, **94**, S Cowley), **always handy, led or
disputed lead from six out, kept on same
pace run-in.** (100/30 op 7/2 tchd 4/1 and 3/1) 3
General Chandos (9-11-10),: 4 Ran. 1½l, 30l.
4m 26.80s (a 24.80s). SR: 49/22/16.
RACECHECK: Wins 2, pl 3, unpl 3.

TARTAN TEMPEST　　　　　　　　7-11-2
0554510F16-B414U2　　　　　　　**G W Richards**
br g Crozier - Frello by Bargello **1988-89** 2¾m h
heavy **(Ayr)**; 2½m h soft **(Carlisle)**
　　1989-90 (Dec) 3m ch good/soft **(Hexham)** nov.
£4,504 (£2,120).

LWR (89+90): **93** (Nk)　　　　　　　TR: **99**

　　March 9, Carlisle, 3m nov chase, soft,
£2,177: 1 Super Fountain (7-10-5), 2 TARTAN
TEMPEST (7-11-3, N Doughty), **patiently
ridden, joined leaders on bit four out, led
after last, soon headed and not quicken.** (9/2
op 4/1) 3 Parson's Cross (6-11-3), 8 OCEANUS
(btn 14l+) (9-10-10, D Shaw), **improved into
midfield halfway, blundered and weakened
six out.** (33/1 op 20/1); 14 Ran. 1½l, 4l, 2½l, 4l,
2l, hd. 6m 38.10s (a 25.10s).
RACECHECK: Wins 0, pl 1, unpl 7.

　　Jan 10, Kelso, 3m nov chase, good to soft,
£2,137: 1 Fish Quay (7-10-10), 2 Ambergate
(9-10-10), 3 Traprain Law (7-11-3), U TARTAN
TEMPEST (7-11-3, G McCourt), **lost place and
behind sixth, blundered and unseated rider
eighth.** (3/1 jt-fav op 5/2); 11 Ran. 1½l, 10l, 15l,
12l, 1½l. 6m 29.30s (a 29.80s).

　　Jan 2, Ayr, 3m 110y nov chase, good to soft,
£2,717: 1 Traprain Law (7-11-5), 2 Radical Lady
(6-11-0), 3 Interim Lib (7-11-5), 4 TARTAN
TEMPEST (7-11-13, G McCourt), **prominent
till outpaced from four out, stayed on from
two out.** (11/8 fav op 5/4 tchd 13/8); 9 Ran. 2½l,
10l, 1½l, hd, 12l. 6m 30.00s (a 26.50s).

ROMANY KING　　　　　　　　　6-11-4
34411-6B21212　　　　　　　　　**G B Balding**
br g Crash Course - Winsome Lady by Tarqogan
1988-89 2m 1f h good/soft **(Devon)**; 2m 1f h soft
(Devon)
　　1989-90 (Feb) 2¼m 110y ch soft **(Fontwell)**
nov; **(Mar)** 2½m ch good/soft **(Chepstow)** nov
Hcp [Open,107,97]. **£9,041 (£6,517).**

LWR (89+90): **97** (2l)　　　　　　　TR: **101**

　　March 22, Devon & Exeter, 2m 1f nov Hcp
chase [Open,101], good to firm, £4,107: 1
Highfire (8-11-2), 2 ROMANY KING (6-11-10,
101, R Guest), **held up, tracked leaders from
five out, close fourth when blundered next,
ridden two out, not quicken.** (6/5 fav op
Evens tchd 4/5) 3 Minim (7-10-5),: 8 Ran. 10l,
nk, 12l, 12l. 4m 25.20s (a 12.20s).
RACECHECK: Wins 2, pl 1, unpl 2.

　　March 10, Chepstow, 2½m nov Hcp chase
[Open,107], good to soft, £4,207: 1 ROMANY
KING (6-11-0, **97**, R Guest), **held up, mistake
12th, led three out, ran on well.** (7/2 tchd 9/2)
2 ASTRE RADIEUX (5-10-10, **93**, S Cowley),
**prominent, led four out to next, every
chance last, ran on.** (6/1 op 4/1) 3 Elvercone
(9-10-12,v), 6 VALASSY (btn 27l) (7-10-13, **99**,
N Williamson,3*), **prominent till hard ridden
and weakened four out.** (14/1) F KILKILMAR-
TIN (8-10-11, **94**, M Richards), **started slowly,
well behind to halfway, good headway,
fourth and running on when fell three out.**
(5/1 op 4/1); 13 Ran. 2l, 7l, 5l, 12l, ¾l, 2l, 2l. 5m
7.50s (a 17.50s). SR: 31/25/20/19/15/6.
RACECHECK: Wins 5, pl 3, unpl 4.

　　March 1, Ludlow, 2½m nov chase, good to
soft, £2,869: 1 Shady Road (8-11-5), 2 RO-
MANY KING (6-11-10, R Guest), **soon behind,
ran on strongly from two out, too much to
do.** (5/2 fav op 9/4 tchd 3/1) 3 Elite Boy
(8-11-12,3*),: 16 Ran. 2l, hd, 15l, 8l, 8l. 5m 7.80s
(a 9.80s). SR: 23/26/30/-/-/-.
RACECHECK: Wins 2, pl 4, unpl 17.

　　Feb 19, Fontwell, 2¼m 110y nov chase, soft,
£2,310: 1 ROMANY KING (6-11-4, R Guest),
**always in touch, challenged from three out,
led last, held on well.** (9/4 fav op 5/2 tchd 3/1)
2 Master Comedy (6-10-11,7*), 3 KILKILMAR-
TIN (8-11-4, M Richards), **behind, headway
and hit 11th, ran on from three out, kept on.**
(33/1 op 20/1); 15 Ran. ¾l, 5l, 3l, ¾l, 2l, 10l, 3l,
8l. 4m 52.30s (a 25.30s).

Figure 18b (continued)

Since the above amounts to a fairly complex selection procedure, the following is a worked example of an actual race, assessed according to its principles. Most gratifyingly the horses indicated as first and second top-rated, Astre Radieux and Romany King, finished first and second to produce a handsome computer straight forecast of £66.23.

Race at Ayr on Friday, 23 April, 1990:

Novices H'cap Chase
2m 5f (£3756) 20 runners

Of these 20 runners, only seven had "Racecheck" entries as part of their past form shown in the *Sporting Life* (see figure 18a, *page 49*). Analysis of this produced the following figures for later computation (see figure 18b, *page 50*).

2.00 (2m 5f Hcap Ch) — **ASTRE RADIEUX** (M Perrett) **8-1, 1; Romany King** (R Guest) **8-1, 2; Bantel Buccaneer** (T Reed) **25-1, 3. Tartan Tempest** (N Doughty) **8-1, 4. 18 ran.** 11-2 JtFav The Humble Tiller, (S Mellor, Swindon) 8, 5. **Tote:** £6.20: £1.50, £1.90, £5.80, £2.00. DF: £7.30. CSF: £66.23. Tricast: £1,415.93. NR: Western Legend, Moiety.

Figure 19

These five figures when subjected to the key-pressing procedure (already described in relation to Only Trouble on page 48) produced the following ratings for the race:

Astre Radieux	36.33 won 8-1
Romany King	33.87 2nd 8-1
Famous Lad	25.49
The Humble Tiller	20.64
Hot Plate	16.58
Tartan Tempest	14.57
Lough Road	6.32

The full result, as given in the *Daily Mail*, was (see figure 19):

I realise, of course, that you may want to use your pocket calculator to make selections by working on ratings that appear, not in specialised racing newspapers, but in daily ones such as the *Daily Mirror*, the *Daily Mail*, the *Sun*, the *Daily Express*, the *Daily Star* or *The Times*.

These publications either fail to give some of the information necessary to amend their own performance ratings so as to take account of race fitness and suitability of course, distance and going in the manner already recommended or make such amendments in an undisclosed manner. However, the backer should amend whatever ratings are featured by applying the same sequence of key-pressing routines that has just been described to what every daily or evening newspaper always includes in its particular coverage of racing – the formlines of individual contestants.

In carrying out this sequence the backer should:

1   Enter the newspaper performance rating for a runner.

2   Press + key.

3   Enter a "betting forecast" figure (10 for a favourite, 9 for a second favourite, etc).

4 Press − key.

5 Enter figure showing horse's finishing position in last race i.e. 1 for a win last time out, 2 for a second last time out etc. N.B. A "duck's egg" (0) should be entered as 7.

6 Press = key.

7 Press × key.

8 From horse's complete formline, enter total number of times horse won or was placed second or third in all races shown in this. If any of these races were run in a previous season they should be included in calculations.

9 Press = key.

10 Press × key.

11 Enter 100.

12 Press ÷ key.

13 Enter total number of digits shown in horse's formline.

14 Press = key.

15 Press √ key.

16 Note down horse's final rating.

Example One: the *Daily Mirror*

This newspaper's race coverage includes "Spotform" ratings which do not appear in a raw form but are already adjusted to take account of such crucial race-day factors as the draw, the going, the distance and the course in question, jockeyship, the trainer's past record and the wearing of blinkers.

With these factors taken into consideration, as well as a runner's recent form and its temperament, the private handicap weights that originally formed the starting-point for Spotform become ratings that have been so finely tuned and adjusted that one horse always emerges as a clearly top-rated selection.

The basic belief of the Spotform team is that whatever a horse has already achieved it may well, given similar circumstances, accomplish again and the singularly refined nature of the final figures they provide means that further adjustments to these should result in some sophisticated final scores.

Spotform ratings are printed on the extreme right of the full form entry for each runner, as can be seen in figure 20 in which Huntworth is top-rated at 36.

2.35 —THE RIP CHASE H'CAP 3m Winner £9,204 (3 run)

1 U11-132 **HUNTWORTH (14)** M Pipe 10 11 10 **(Gd, Fm, Sft, CD, BF)**....................A Walter 36●
Won here 3m October. Rallied to get within 1½l of Mr Frisk 3m Sandown
2 1352-12 **IMADYNA (NZ) (28)** D Barons 8 10 12 **(Gd, Fm, C, BF)**.................. *R Greene 33
No extra on the flat when 11 2nd to Karakter Reference at Kempton
3 U43-3F4 **NAUTICAL JOKE (7)** W Stephenson 11 10 8 **(Gd, Sft, Hy, Fm, D, SF)**
C Grant —
Would win this on best form, but 2 efforts this term not encouraging
Betting: 11-10 Huntworth. 11-8 Imadyna. 7-2 Nautical Joke.

Figure 20

If you now apply the 16-stage key-pressing routine already described to the ratings given to Huntworth and Imadyna, you should find that the former, with 60.55, came out better than the latter with 57.73.

Interestingly, in the event, Huntworth won at 11-8 from Imadyna at 13-8 with the unrated Nautical Joke finishing third (see figure 21).

2.35 (3m handicap chase, £9,204.00)
1 **HUNTWORTH,** Mr A Walter 11-8 Fav
2 IMADYNA (NZ), R Greene 13-8
3 NAUTICAL JOKE, C Grant 3-1
3 ran. Dist: 7 7. M Pipe, Nicolashayne. Tote:
win £1.90. DF: £1.70. CSF: £3.44.

Figure 21

Example Two: the *Daily Mail*

In his widely read guide to horse-race selection and betting, author Peter Braddock recommends the *Daily Mail* for the excellence of its racing coverage, of which an impressive part is represented by "Formcast" – a set of private handicap ratings.

Figure 22

As it happens, I have kept a now-yellowing copy of an article on Formcast in which it is claimed that its ratings are likely to work out best in races carrying the most prize money. Thus, on any race-day, I always rate the most valuable race at a meeting that Formcast has rated – a procedure true to the very first principle of race selection already discussed. Consequently, on the very day that Huntworth won at Ascot, I noticed that the H & T Walker Gold Cup was actually, with its penalty value of £21,300, the most valuable race on the

```
2.05 (2m 4f Grade 2 h'cap chase, £21,300.00)
1 BLAZING WALKER, C Grant 7-2
2 FULL STRENGTH, N Doughty 10-3
3 MULTUM IN PARVO, N Williamson 13-8 Fav
5 ran. Dist: 3 25 3 20. W A Stephenson, Bishop
Auckland. Tote: win £4.10 places £1.80 £1.80.
DF: £6.90. CSF: £13.81.
```

Figure 23

six-race card at this meeting (see figures 22 and 23).

Using the Formcast figures given above as starting points and following the very same 16-step sequence of computational stages, as featured in previous adjustments to Spotform ratings, I produced these final figures for this Grade II steeplechase:

Cashew King	68.79
Blazing Walker	91.65
Multum in Parvo	85.14
Full Strength	90.55
Sire Nantais	63.24

Incredibly, the race was won by the 7-2 chance, and appropriately named, Blazing Walker from Full Strength at 100-30 with the disappointing 13-8 favourite Multum in Parvo third and I thus collected a handsome computer straight forecast dividend of £13.81.

Example Three: the *Sun*

The large circulation of this newspaper means that it is consulted by many a fan of horse-racing. Thus, it is fortunate that within its pages, the "Sport of Kings" is given comprehensive and uncontroversial coverage.

As for this particular paper's form services, the first of these, "Sun Form" is a concise and fairly extensive form summary which usefully incorporates race-readers' comments.

Even more usefully for those interested in computa-tional approaches to winner-finding, a further form service known as "Sunratings" accords a score of 99 (as in its Murdoch stable-mate *The Times*) to a runner top-rated according to this particular private handicap whose ratings have, on occasion, proved highly accurate. Indeed, from 9 November 1987, to the 23 March 1988, Sunratings allegedly top-rated 1,057 horses of which 407, or 38 per cent, were actually successful.

A possible way of improving on such blanket success is to amend Sunratings in exactly the same way as were their equivalents in the *Daily Mirror* and the *Daily Mail* – by the same 16-stage process already described.

Example Four: the *Daily Express*

This newspaper is particularly useful to the serious follower of horse-racing, since it is the only non-specialist newspaper that features the selections of both the private handicapper responsible for the W

Figure 24

'Deep Sensation'

factor service and an assessor of race times and is also the only newspaper that additionally features the choices of a computer programmer.

As it happens, on the same day as W factor, this newspaper's private handicapper, had also selected Huntworth, I also concentrated on the claims of Warwick runner Deep Sensation (given a massive rating of 143). When the W factor ratings for these horses were adjusted by the now-familiar, 16-step process, Deep Sensation was selected to carry the cash. In the event he won readily at 10-11 (see figures 24 and 25).

```
1.00 (2m hurdle, £3,556.25)
1 DEEP SENSATION, R Rowe 10-11 Fav
2 ATLAAL, M Ahern 14-1
3 SPRING HAY, R Dunwoody 7-4
9 ran. Dist: ¾ 15 ½ 25 15.
J Gifford, Findon.
Tote: win £1.90 places £1.40 £1.90 £1.10. DF:
£11.50. CSF: £12.69.
```

Figure 25

Example Five: the *Daily Star*

Since the *Daily Star* bills itself as the newspaper that's "light years ahead", it is not surprising that it offers readers of its racing page something rather distinctive, if not exactly "out of sight". Indeed, the ratings appended to the names of many of the day's runners are the only ones published in a national daily which are based on time rather than past form. This, in fact,

Figure 26

explains why these ratings sometimes diverge so much from those of other newspaper form experts, amongst whom there is often a broad consensus as to runners "best in" at the weights.

The "Clockform" ratings in the *Daily Star* are, in fact, supplied by Split Second, the time expert of Raceform's weekly Update, but for the particular benefit of *Daily Star* readers, horses that have not previously run fast enough to be accorded a (lowly) speed figure of 40 are given a rating based on "recent form and other factors".

```
1.15 (3m 110yds handicap chase, £3,785.00)
1 CARRICK HILL LAD, G McCourt 8-11 Fav
2 BIRLING JACK, P Niven 7-2
3 FOUR TRIX, D Byrne 3-1
5 ran. Dist: 12 1½ 4 30. G Richards,
Greystoke. Tote: win £1.50 places £1.40
£1.80. DF: £2.70. CSF: £3.65.
```

Figure 27

Any agreement in the *Daily Star* between Clockform and Starform should indicate horses whose form may well be worth subjecting to further computation. On the same test day that the two "great minds" responsible for these features put *Daily Star* readers on to several other winners such as Huntworth, they also pinpointed the chances of Carrick Hill Lad. With a top-rating (amended by calculator) to 85.44 he duly trotted up by 12 lengths at 8-11.

Example Six: *The Times*

Lastly, it would seem appropriate that in a final bid to help you refine the ratings offered in the various

'Heavyweight rivals'

racing-pages of daily newspapers, I try to go out with a bang by suggesting how those of the "Thunderer" might be profitably exploited by adjusting them on a pocket calculator. In my view, *The Times* gives racing even more serious coverage than some of its heavyweight rivals.

One top people's plan that may prove more lucrative than my past attempts to win Portfolio – this newspaper's upmarket bingo game – involves computing the chances of the runners in the particular race that is to be contested by the nap selection of *The Times*' private handicapper. If his selection duly emerges as still top-rated, once the 16-stage amendment procedure has been completed, then you may well have found something to bet on.

This was certainly the case on the same day the victories of Huntworth, Deep Sensation and Carrick Hill Lad had occurred. Before this had ended I had seen that the horse accorded the distinction of being the top-rated selection of *The Times*' private handicapper had also come out best (with a rating of 94.42) on my calculator. This was Elder Prince and, thankfully, it also won by three lengths at 11-10.

2.45 MONTGOMERIE HANDICAP HURDLE (£2,709: 2m) (6 runners)

1	0211-2F	CANDLEBRIGHT 35 (BF,CD,F,G,S) (Western Owners) G Richards 6-11-10....	G McCourt	91
2	613-211	ELDER PRINCE 4 (D,F,S) (W Pratt) M H Easterby 4-11-3 (4ex).................	L Wyer ●	99
3	11060-	SKOLERN 173F (CD,F,G) (I Greaves) A Harrison 6-10-12	M Dwyer	87
4	516-021	CLAY COUNTY 35 (CD,G,S) (M Boyd) R Allan 5-10-9........................	B Storey	94
5	1/	BELDINE 11F (D,F) (W Monteith) P Monteith 5-10-4....................	L O'Hara (3)	—
6	0/56355-	REGAL ESTATE 262 (S) (I Ives) D Moffatt 6-10-2..........................	D J Moffatt (7)	90

BETTING: 2-1 Clay County, 5-2 Elder Prince, 9-2 Candlebright, 7-1 Skolern, 10-1 others.

1989: ALBERT THE GREAT 6-9-11 D Byrne (14-1) P Liddle 13 ran

The Times Private Handicapper's top rating: 2.45 **ELDER PRINCE.**

Figure 28

2.45 (2m handicap hurdle, £2,709.00)
1 ELDER PRINCE, L Wyer 11-10 Fav
2 REGAL ESTATE, D J Moffatt 25-1
3 SKOLERN, J Callaghan 6-1
5 ran. Dist: 3 10 20 4. M H Easterby, Great Habton. Tote: win £1.70 places £1.20 £3.20.
DF: £15.90. CSF: £17.24. NR: Candlebright.

Figure 29

CHAPTER 3

Calculating when to bet from betting shows

Having used a calculator to select the race on any racing-day that is most suitable for investment purposes and actually to make a selection in this, the backer should again employ electronics to calculate exactly when to make a wager.

Interestingly, *When To Bet And Win* was the name given to a once-best-selling work which advised backers how to do so, and I can only endorse the view of its author that, if they know *when* to get involved, backers can exercise the same businesslike control over their activities that is the cornerstone of successful bookmaking.

As was recently pointed out in an advertisement for a "revolutionary new concept in betting", in the business transacted between backers and bookmakers, the latter have a built-in advantage. This is, of course, generally so and helps to explain why, in archetypal terms, bookmakers have long, if rather erroneously, been seen as cigar-smoking, rather flashily dressed and ostentatiously wealthy owners of large cars with

'Flashy bookies'

personalised number plates.

However, the racing enthusiast must be aware of the methods of the bookmaker. If you are "armed" with your pocket calculator in betting shops, on racecourses or in your armchair, you can rapidly check the prices that make up each successive betting show and so determine when a book – that is, a complete set of prices for a race – is no longer excessively or unfairly "over-round".

The calculations concerned here involved dividing

the right-hand side of each runner's odds by the sum of both sides. Thus, 7-4 becomes 4÷11. Separate calculations need to be made for every runner in the race and the resultant decimal fractions added together to give a final total.

An example from an actual race is given in figure 30.

Odds	Calculation needed	Result
6−4	4÷10	0.4000
11−4	4÷15	0.2667
7−2	2÷9	0.2222
6−1	1÷7	0.1429
25−1	1÷26	0.0385
	Total	1.0703

Figure 30

The result, after moving the decimal point two places to the right, is 107.03. Thus, the bookmaker is working to 107 per cent. His book is 7 per cent "over-round" and he is offering backers overall value for money since a book that is only "over-round" by 15 per cent or less is a rather rare circumstance and one that is most likely to arise when prices are being quoted against the runners in a small field. (Often in races in which a large field faces the starter, the odds quoted against the chances of fancied contestants may be reasonably tempting, yet outsiders could well be on offer at very cramped rates. What frequently results is a book that is excessively and quite unfairly "over-round".)

'If you are armed'

If degrees of "over-roundness" under 15 per cent are discovered by this rapid calculation, you should waste no time in "getting on" before, as is fairly likely, the trading position becomes far less favourable. Very often it will be found that bookmakers (who work to marked cards indicating by means of a cross, a dot and a capital C, the likely first and second favourites and a third runner about which they are warned to be "careful") recognise their initial vulnerability and so start to trade at rates that are distinctly ungenerous. Frequently, the opening show will, in fact, feature prices that prove to be "over-round" by well over 20 per cent.

If this is the case, you should patiently note the opening prices and hope for some overall improvement in the trading position. This will often occur, as is illustrated in figure 31 which shows exactly how the odds quoted against the runners in an actual eight-horse race fluctuated between the first show and the close of trading. It provides most convincing proof of the wisdom of using an electronic calculator in an attempt to play and, with luck, beat the bookmakers at their own "numbers game".

Some backers who are of the opinion that when money "talks" in racing it does so just as revealingly as

	Odds at first show		Odds at final show	
A	4−7	63.64*	4−5	55.56*
B	7−2	22.22	9−2	18.18
C	5−1	16.67	7−1	12.50
D	5−1	16.67	9−1	10.00
E	16−1	5.88	12−1	7.67
F	16−1	5.88	25−1	3.85
G	16−1	5.88	25−1	3.85
H	20−1	4.76	33−1	2.94
	Total	141.60	Total	114.55
	Over-round	41.60	Over-round	14.55

Figure 31 (After division process and moving decimal point two places to right)

it does in many other spheres of human activity, may wish to use their calculators to determine from betting shows, rather than from racing form, precisely which contender to support.

Firstly, it should be pointed out that if on the racetrack, or on a television screen at home, or in a betting shop, or at a greyhound stadium, backers notice that only *one* of two clear market leaders (preferably the favourite since possession of this much-vaunted status is usually sufficient to produce a great deal of imitative, as opposed to inspired, support) has its odds only marginally trimmed and an outsider has its opening odds cut considerably (i.e. by a very large proportion) they may have spotted a potentially most favourable development, as in the race return shown in figure 32.

```
        PELERIN (FR) 4-8-8 B Taylor (5th st,
          swtchd ins 1f out, sqzd thro and
          led cl home) .......................................  1
     51*CRACAVAL 5-8-8 S Cauthen (lw outpcd,
          gd hdwy 2f out, ev ch ins fnl f. r.o.) ... hd—2
        SHINING FINISH 4-8-11 P. Eddery (lw,
          4th st, led 2f out, led over 1f out,
          hard  rdn,  r.o.) .................................. hd—3
     51 SON FILS 6-8-8 G Starkey (hdwy 3f out,
          led wl over 1f out, not qckn fnl f) ...... 2½—4
        SHAFTESBURY 5-8-8 W R Swinburn (bit
          bkwd, 2nd st. led over 3f out, wknd
          1f out)  .............................................. 3—5
        NICHOLAS BILL 5-9-0 P Waldron (lw, 6th
          st, ev ch 2f out, onecpd( ..................  10—6
        LIGHT CAVALRY (fav) 4-9-0 L Piggot (3rd st
          rdn and wknd over 2f out) ......................  7
        SACRILEGE 5-8-8 N Day (lw, led over 8f) ...  8
        SHOOT A LINE 4-8-11 W Carson (hit stalls,
          a wl bhd, virt p.u. 3f out) ......................  9
     5/2 L Cavalry (3's), 3 S A Line (9/4), 4 Cracaval
     (7/2, 5 N Bill 8 S Finish, 16 PELERIN (20's), 25
          Shaftesbury, 33 S Fils, 66 Sacrilege.
```

Figure 32

As can be seen, Pelerin advanced in the betting against his opening odds of 20-1 – a contraction (calculated as representing 20 per cent) – that transpired by virtue, not of the imitative behaviour that so characterises the backers of favourites, but quite conceivably because of the fairly heavy weight of genuinely inspired support for this eventual long-priced winner.

In this often crucial business of determining which horse is actually causing bookmakers to revise their initial estimate of its chances more radically than is the case with any other runner, a calculator becomes necessary because, on occasion, you have the tricky task of deciding whether the most "trimmed" runner is, say, a 6-4 favourite shortening to 11-8 or a 7-2 shot falling to 3-1.

In the former example (as in all calculations that involve different digits featuring on the right-hand sides of the two rates of odds in question) you first have to find a common denominator for these. For the 4 and the 8 in the odds of 6-4 and 11-8 this is obviously 8. Thus it could be said that 12/8ths (6-4) had contracted to 11/8ths – a reduction of one-twelfth or, as your calculator will reveal, of 8.5 per cent. In the case of 7-2 contracting to 3-1 this is seven "halves" contracting to six – a reduction of one-seventh, or of 14.28 per cent. Thus, the latter contraction emerges as the greater and, possibly, the more significant.

CHAPTER 4

Calculating what outsiders to support

In the wake of the stock market crash of 1988, the great hurricane of the same year and the San Francisco earthquake a year later, came a renewed interest in catastrophe theory that was first formulated in 1965 by the distinguished French mathematician René Thom.

Since Thom's theory of chaos is mathematical in nature it would seem sensible to use a pocket calculator's capacity to process numerical variables in a brave attempt to bring some order into the chaos that racing can seem to represent when results of races suddenly feature a high incidence of successful outsiders.

Catastrophe theorists might well attribute such sudden alterations from the usual equine behaviour that expert judges, bookmakers and the majority of backers have expected, to radical changes in those influences that have previously governed this behaviour. Since in racing the state of the going is one of these influences, when this changes from a sound, reliable surface to one that is treacherous, heavy or soft, it is time to use your calculator to predict the effect that the opening of the heavens can have on horses' racing form.

Research has, in fact, shown that, as might be expected, horses (like Little Polveir, the horse that won the 1989 Grand National) of proven stamina that carry lightish weights over the heavy or soft ground on which they have previously prevailed often win highly competitive long-distance races at long odds that fail to reflect the fact that, prior to these victories, they ran on unsuitably good or firm ground.

Thus, when it is noticed that the going has suddenly changed from good or firm to soft or (preferably) heavy, it is time to reach for a calculator and to try to predict precisely which horse may well cause a form upset or "catastrophe".

In detail this involves assigning those horses that are due to contest the day's longest race on soft or heavy ground, points according to the following factors:

1. their positions in the betting;
2. their positions in the weights;
3. their proven ability to win over the distance in question;
4. their possible past successes on the course on which they are due to compete;
5. their possible past successes on the going;
6. the numerical strength of the opposition they face.

Here, the calculations needed (using the memory + key throughout) involve assigning the runners scores according to figure 33.

Thus, a maximum-rated outsider would receive 60 points for being quoted as 10th or even further "out

Points to be awarded for each of factors 1-6	Factor 1: position in betting	Factor 2: position in weights	Factor 3: successes over distance	Factor 4: past wins on course	Factor 5: past wins on prevailing going	Factor 6: number of runners
10	10th or higher	10th "top" (or even lower down)	3 or more past wins	3 or more past wins	3 or more past wins	50 or more
9	9th	9th "top"				
8	8th	8th "top"				40-49
7	7th	7th "top"				
6	6th	6th "top"	2 past wins	2 past wins	2 past wins	30-39
5	5th	5th "top"				
4	4th	4th "top"				20-29
3	3rd	3rd "top"				
2	2nd	2nd "top"	1 past win	1 past win	1 past win	10-19
1	1st	Top weight				

Figure 33

SEAGRAM GRAND NATIONAL H'CAP CHASE   £66840   4m 4f

2377 **LITTLE POLVEIR** (G B Balding) 12-10-3(3ow)(10oh) J Frost 28/1: 52403541: '2 b g Cantab - Blue Speedwell (Escart III) Smart chaser who returned to his very best when successful in the Grand National at Liverpool: 10lbs out of the h'cap but led ½ way, jumped well and stayed on strongly on this searching run-in: tried in bl last time but much btr without them: recently joined current stable (prev trained by J Edwards): first time out won a minor event at Fontwell in Oct: in '87/8 won h'caps at Nottingham and Devon (rtd 80): prev season lifted the Scottish National at Ayr: eff 3m2f, well suited by extreme dist and is an out-and-out stayer: acts on fast grnd, likes yldg or soft/hvy.

2448 **WEST TIP** (M Oliver) 12-10-11 R Dunwoody 12/1: 43-F5152:   Nicely bckd from 20/1: always cl-up, stayed on v well: has tremendous record in this race: winner in '86, fourth in '87 and again in '88: see 2300.

2448 **THE THINKER** (W Stephenson) 11-11-10 S Sherwood 10/1: 11/113F3: Went from ½ way: blun and lost place 9 out, staying on again when another blun 2 out ended his hopes: grand effort under topweight: see 1181.

2199 **LASTOFTHEBROWNIES** (M Morris) 9-10-0 T Carmody 16/1: 22050434: Prom from ½ way, stayed on: ran well in the race last year and is a sound jumper of these big fences: see 884.

*2478 **DURHAM EDITION** 11-10-11 C Grant 15/2: -3555215: Very well bckd: steady prog from ½ way, chall last but wknd flat, as he did last season: another fine effort: see 2478.

2244 **MONANORE** 12-10-6(3ow) G Mccourt 20/1: -5006106: Always prom, onepace from 4 out: see 1189, 2244.

2449 **GALAS IMAGE** 9-10-3(2ow) N Doughty 18/1: 60342227: Cl-up a mile from home, wknd 4 out: see 714, 2449

2448 **BONANZA BOY** 8-11-1 P Scudamore 10/1: 0-11F148: Went prom ½ way, wknd 3 out: very hard race 2218

2432 **TEAM CHALLENGE** 7-10-0(bl)(16oh) M Bowlby 30/1: 3-414339: Prom till wknd last: gd run at the weights: now wears blinkers: see 1170: stays long distances.

--   **NEWNHAM** 12-10-5(5ow) Mr S R Andrews 50/1: 2/3100-0: Lost touch after 3m, fin 10th: recent point-to-point winner: rtd 65c when a narrow winner of the Fox Hunters Chase over these fences in '87/8: failed to re-produce that form in his 2 subs starts last term: eff over 2m6f, stays long dist: gd jumper who acts on fast & yld.

2252 **THE THIRSTY FARMER** 10-10-2(bl)(2ow)(38oh) L Kelp 100/1: -2600650: Very s;iff task: prom over 3m, fin 11th: has recently joined the M Pipe stable: rtd 46c back in 600.

Figure 34

74

2242 **ATTITUDE ADJUSTER** 9-10-6(bl)(6ow)(11oh) N Madden 25/1: /65-0260: Always in rear after bad early blun: fin a remote 12th: **see 2242, 2195.**

*2640 **SIDBURY HILL** 13-10-0(35oh) K Mooney 100/1: 4-253310: T.o. from ½ way: very stiff task: **see 2640.**

2242 **MR BAKER** 11-10-0(15oh) M Moran 100/1: -4004100: Sn well behind: last of the 14 to finish: Irish challenger who gained sole success this term in a modest h'cap at Tremore in Jan (2m6f, hvy): revels in the mud: stays at least 3m: all winning form on sharp trks.

*2449 **DIXTON HOUSE** 10-10-3(3ow) T Morgan 7/1 FAV: 0121/21F: Heavily bckd fav: fell Bechers 1st time.

1939 **PERRIS VALLEY** 8-10-0 B Sheridan 16/1: 11-F56PF: Irish chall: rear when fell 11th: **see 884.**

2449 **SMART TAR** 8-10-3 C Llewellyn 18/1: -302264U: Prom when u.r. 11 out: best 1142.

*2510 **STEARSBY** 10-10-9 B Powell 14/1: 0F-R221R: Nicely bckd: made most till ref 11th.

2575 **Sir Jest** 11-10-1(1ow)(7oh) U   2360 **Beamwam** 11-10-6(6ow)(13oh) P   2510 **Queensway Boy** 10-10-0(7oh) R

1939 **Sergeant Sprite** 9-10-2(2ow)(11oh) U   2445 **Bartres** 10-10-3(3ow)(14oh) P

2449 **Galnay** 10-10-6(bl)(6ow)(8oh) F   2710 **Memberson** 11-10-2(2ow)(4oh) P

2432 **Bob Tisdall** 10-10-7 R   2431 **Seeandem** 9-10-0(17oh) F   2619 **Cerimau** 11-10-0(20oh) F

2406 **Rausal** 10-10-0(21oh) R   2444 **Friendly Henry** 9-10-4(4ow)(26oh) F

*2467 **Mithras** 11-10-1(1ow)(26oh) P   2681 **Polar Nomad** 8-10-0(25oh) P   2082 **Numerate** 10-10-0(27oh) P

2569 **Hettinger** 9-10-0(28oh) F   2584 **Kersil** 12-10-0(32oh) P   2595 **Brown Trix** 11-10-5(5ow)(22oh) F

2242 **Craniome** 11-10-0(6oh) F   *2843 **Mearlin** 10-10-0(38oh) P   1063 **Smartside** 14-10-5(5ow)(46oh) R

2632 **Mr Chris** 10-10-0(46oh) F

40 ran   Dists. 7, ¾, 6, 5, 8, 2½, 1¼4, 15   (Mr Edward Harvey)   G Balding Fyfield, Hants.

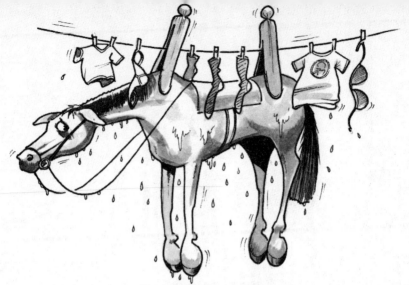

'Out with the washing'

with the washing" in the betting forecast, for being 10th or even lower in the weights, for having won at least three times over the distance, for having been as successful on the course and on the prevailing soft or heavy ground, and for having 50 or more rivals.

One horse that in the 1989 Grand National came quite close to receiving such a maximum score was Little Polveir. This staying chaser was given 38 points – 10 for being quoted beyond 10th and so "out with the washing" in the betting, 10 for having registered more than three previous wins on wet ground, eight for being part of a 40-strong field, and 10 for being weighted lower than 10th in the weights. Thus he became a confident "top-rated" selection that the calculator placed well clear even of West Tip – the only horse in the race to be accorded any points for both notching a previous distance win and doing so over Aintree's four-and-a-half mile Grand National course. Despite carrying three pounds overweight, Little Polveir ran out a most convincing seven-length winner at 28-1.

CHAPTER 5

Calculating what to bet by computing greyhound racing form

The imponderable that is represented by a contest for unraced two-year-old racehorses has no equivalent in greyhound racing and this is just one reason why this sport is ideally suitable for winner-finding by calculator. The fact that the National Greyhound Racing Club insists that no dog or bitch can race until it has run three official trials means that the form of greyhounds is far more exposed than that of many racehorses, and this is yet another reason why the assessment of greyhounds' winning prospects lends itself so readily to computation by calculator. Another is that, thanks to the continuing rivalry between the *Racing Post* and the *Sporting Life*, the modern-day follower of Britain's second most popular spectator sport has never been so well armed to battle with the bookmakers, such is the wealth of information and detailed statistical analysis of past form now at his disposal.

My extensive research into which factors can exert influences on the outcomes of greyhound races suggests that, as with horse-racing, one of the most critical is the type of race in question.

It is first wise to discount the (far from numerous) handicap races for greyhounds and to concentrate your attention on non-handicap contests which, unless open events, are divided into certain grades which range from 1 to 8 in descending order of class. Thus, an A1 race is for top-class sprinters, an S5 event for middle-of-the-road stayers, and an M8 contest is one for novices racing over middle-range distances.

2.37			(523 metres M5)				£44
Trap 1—BEGGARS BALL bk b Game Ball — Hollands Kay 2/87 (9/4/89)							**Maxen**
20 Mr	523 1	6.10	1st	1¼ Easy Captain led run in 32.68	+20	7-2	M5 32.88
13 Mr	523 2	6.12	3rd	2½ Catch Lucky ev ch 32.56	+10	8-1	M5 32.86
10 Mr	523 1	6.10	1st	2 HIDE JET led run in 32.64	+20	7-2	M6 32.84
6 Mr	523 2	6.01	1st	Hd Poor Old Fred fin well.............32.75	+20	7-2	M6 32.95
Trap 2—POUND FOOLISH w bk b Ballregan Bob — Celtic Aran 2/88							**Greenacre**
20 Mr	523 3	6.09	5th	4¼ Beggars Ball b blk 1 ....32.68	+20	12-1	M5 33.23
13 Mr	523 3	6.17	5th	4½ Catch Lucky ev ch 32.56	+10	7-1	M5 33.02
8 Mr	523 3	6.12	4th	5¾ Hard To Live b crd to 1 ....32.38	+20	4-1	M5 33.05
1 Mr	523 3	6.27	5th	4¾ Clune Spinner ev ch 32.48	+10	7-4F	M5 32.96
Trap 3—MY TITAN w bk d Master Stack — Night Horizon 2/87							**Walsh**
13 Mr	523 4	6.25	2nd	2½ Robos Revenge wide 4 bmpd ran on ...33.31	+10	11-8F	M6 33.61
6 Mr	523 3	6.08	3rd	3¼ Beggars Ball eased 3 ....32.75	+20	13-8F	M6 33.21
1 Mr	523 2	6.13	6th	4¾ Clune Spinner handy to 3 ....32.48	+10	10-1	M5 32.97
15 Fb	523 3	6.33	3rd	5¾ Dutchmans Nippy ev ch 32.84	-10	5-1	M5 33.20
Trap 4—SLANEMORE ROCKET (W) bd d Game Man — Munsboro Pa 4/87							**Chandler**
8 Mr	523 5	6.10	3rd	2½ Hard To Live ev ch 32.33	+20	9-4F	M5 32.79
3 Mr	523 6	6.15	5th	1½ Tornaroy Hall crd 1 ....32.93	+10	6-4F	M5 33.15
1 Mr	523 4	6.01	2nd	2¼ Clune Spinner q a led to 2 ....32.48	+10	4-1	M5 32.76
17 Fb	523 4	6.01	3rd	2¼ Tornaroy Hall showed to 3 ....32.73	-10	4-1	M5 32.82
Trap 5—ROBOS REVENGE (W) w bk d Sand Man — Andy'S Lighthouse 5/87							**Bateman**
13 Mr	523 6	6.09	1st	2½ My Titan e p led 1 ....33.31	+10	5-1	M6 33.41
6 Mr	523 5	6.00	6th	10¼ Beggars Ball crd 1 ....32.75	+20	7-1	M6 33.77
20 Fb	523 4	6.04	4th	7¼ Easy Captain ev ch 33.00	-20	9-2	M6 33.38
13 Fb	523 5	5.87	1st DHT	Pound Foolish al led held on 33.09	N	8-1	M6 33.09
Trap 6—PASHA LASS (W) f b Whisper Wishes — Ballyhaden Queen 8/88							**Tite**
20 Mr	523 6	6.13	1st	Nk Bob The Poacher wide led n/l 33.05	N	3-1	M6 33.05
13 Mr	523 5	6.16	4th	5 Robos Revenge b blk 1 and 4 ....33.31	+10	5-2	M6 33.81
10 Mr	523 5	6.14	4th	5½ Beggars Ball b blk 1 ....32.64	+20	9-2	M6 33.28
6 Mr	484 5	4.13	3rd	1½ Ardbeg Support s a ran on 30.49	+20	4-1	A8 30.81

BETTING: 6-4 Beggars Ball, 15-8 Slanemore Rocket, 6 Pound Foolish, Pasha Lass, 12 My Titan, Robos Revenge

Sel: BEGGARS BALL D.: Slanemore Rocket F.Alt: Pound Foolish

1 **Beggars Ball**—*drawn well, quick double on the cards, stays*
2 **Pound Foolish**—*middle tracker, plenty of luck needed to score*
3 **My Titan**—*unimpressive in recent outings, runs on*
4 **Slanemore Rocket**—*push nose in front by the turn, has to be caught*
5 **Robos Revenge**—*loves to dictate, four likely to fill that roll*
6 **Pasha Lass**—*takes a step up in company after narrow victory, wide*

Figure 35

HACKNEY CLOCKWORK

The figure following the greyhound's name is the runner's basic points ratings, based mainly on recent performance. The next column provides for a grading allowance - not applicable in opens or intertracks - to cater for a rise or fall in grade. The trap bonus is Clockwork's personal assessment on the make-up of the race, with the best-drawn runner receiving six points, the next best drawn five, etc. The final column represents the greyhound's final points tally: with the selection (in capitals) being the runner with the most number of points.

	Basic Points	Grading Allows.	Trap Bonus	Rating
2.03				
1 Ivy Francis	40	-	3	43
2 Black Hannah	63	S	4	67
3 Howardstown Giro	32	S	1	33
4 Road To Cahir	47	S	2	49
5 Strong Belief	43	S	5	48
6 DEMES PURSUIT	68	+8	6	82
2.19				
1 Jumping Bing	84	S	5	89
2 Monroe Slipper	68	+8	1	77
3 Tracton Dasher	59	+8	4	71
4 Howardstown Band	75	S	2	77
5 OYSTER NANCY	88	+8	3	99
6 Michaels Dog	70	S	6	76
2.37				
1 Beggars Ball	55	S	6	61
2 Pound Foolish	53	S	2	55
3 My Titan	43	-8	1	36
4 SLANEMORE ROCKET	64	S	5	69
5 Robos Revenge	30	-8	4	26
6 Pasha Lass	35	-8	3	30
2.52				
1 One To Beat	52	-8	6	50
2 ARDBEG SUP-PORT	70	S	5	75
3 More By Luck	61	S	1	62
4 Killimy Jet	57	S	4	61
5 Beechill Bandit	61	S	3	64
6 Hide Jet	61	S	2	63

3.11			
1 Easy Tan	77	S	6	83
2 POKER LORD	81	S	5	86
3 Bridin Fountain	82	S	1	83
4 Well Reared	74	S	2	76
5 Kittys Rogue	70	-16	4	58
6 Direct Victory	75	S	3	78
3.29			
1 Hopeful Easy	104	-8	4	100
2 Black Sovereign	97	-8	5	94
3 Wishes Corner	88	-8	1	81
4 MA DOYLE	122	S	3	125
5 Dilly's Fella	122	S	2	124
6 Slippy Supreme	102	-8	6	100
3.49			
1 MACAMORE CHAMP	86	S	6	92
2 Janice Karen	65	+8	2	75
3 Hard To Live	82	-8	3	77
4 Kanavaun	57	-	1	58
5 Midway Girl	30	-	5	35
6 Move Over Sandra	76	+8	4	88
4.05			
1 Bing Crest	95	S	6	101
2 Gone North	88	S	4	92
3 Tracton Boss	82	S	2	84
4 HARRYS BULLET	111	S	3	114
5 Minane Band	99	S	1	100
6 White Cloud	100	S	5	105
4.22			
1 Chrysos	93	-16	5	82
2 ELTONS WEL-COME	122	S	4	126
3 Floras Darkie	90	-24	1	67
4 Skevanish Fox	102	+8	6	116
5 Tracton Wonder	88	S	3	91
6 Exchange Fosters	113	S	2	115
4.37			
1 Bar Of Steel	104	S	6	110
2 NELSONS COBRA	134	S	3	137
3 Egmont Bam-beano	111	+8	2	121
4 Slaneyside Beech	118	+8	4	130
5 Coal Bucket	104	S	1	105
6 Orlando Sand	111	S	5	116

Figure 36

4.55						5.10				
1 Catch Lucky	74	-16	4	62		1 My Apologies	90	-8	6	88
2 Sheanabog	79	S	6	85		2 Regiment Squire	86	-8	2	80
3 Grandads Image	82	S	1	83		3 Moonlight Susie	79	S	5	84
4 DRUMNA TEAK	97	S	5	102		4 Ice Cap	66	-	1	67
5 FAST JAZZ	100	S	2	102		5 Donnas Model	79	S	3	82
6 Basils Cossie	68	S	3	71		6 GIVE ME FIVE	104	S	4	108

Figure 36 (continued)

PERFORMANCE POINTERS

COMPUTED PERFORMANCES AT HACKNEY (since 1/1/88)

2.03 (484m A8)	Total W-R	Per cent	£1 Level Stake	Trap Record	A8 Races	Since Win
Trap 1 - IVY FRANCIS	2-15	13.3	- 7.50	1-7	0-0	3
Trap 2 - BLACK HANNAH	0-6	-	- 6.00	0-0	0-4	-
Trap 3 - HOWARDSTOWN GIRO	0-1	-	- 1.00	0-0	0-1	-
Trap 4 - ROAD TO CAHIR	0-5	-	- 5.00	0-2	0-5	-
Trap 5 - STRONG BELIEF	0-11	-	- 11.00	0-5	0-5	-
Trap 6 - DEMES PURSUIT	0-5	-	- 5.00	0-1	0-1	-
2.19 (484m A7)	Total W-R	Per cent	£1 Level Stake	Trap Record	A7 Races	Since Win
Trap 1 - JUMPING BING	3-22	13.6	- 5.75	3-14	2-10	7
Trap 2 - MONROE SLIPPER	0-2	-	- 2.00	0-0	0-0	-
Trap 3 - TRACTON DASHER	9-47	19.1	- 6.12	4-23	3-9	1
Trap 4 - HOWARDSTOWN BAND	1-3	33.3	- 0.75	1-2	0-2	1
Trap 5 - OYSTER NANCY	3-19	15.8	+ 1.25	2-7	1-9	3
Trap 6 - MICHAELS DOG	1-10	10.0	- 7.00	0-2	0-5	7
2.37 (523m M5)	Total W-R	Per cent	£1 Level Stake	Trap Record	M5 Races	Since Win
Trap 1 - BEGGARS BALL	7-40	17.5	- 11.50	2-5	1-18	0
Trap 2 - POUND FOOLISH	2-14	14.3	- 8.00	0-1	0-5	4
Trap 3 - MY TITAN	5-32	15.6	- 1.50	2-14	0-10	5
Trap 4 - SLANEMORE ROCKET	2-16	12.5	- 10.25	0-4	0-8	4
Trap 5 - ROBOS REVENGE	3-8	37.5	+ 6.50	1-4	0-0	0
Trap 6 - PASHA LASS	1-4	25.0	0.00	1-1	0-0	0

Figure 37

While some judges make general statements that winners are easier to find if you avoid both top-class (grade 1 or 2) events and those (in grades 7 and 8) for novices, my preference, which is surely more logical, is for a race in which the six dogs concerned can be seen (from the four-line summaries of their most recent

81

Dog number	Enter "Clockwork's" "trap suitability" rating	Enter points for most recent time	Enter speed to first bend rating	Enter class rating for any recent placings in last four runs	Enter 96 as optimum class rating for last four outings	Final rating after computing these figures
1 Beggar's Ball	6	5	3	40	96	18.25
2 Pound Foolish	2	3	5	0	96	—
3 My Titan	1	1	4	25	96	—
4 Slanemore Rocket	5	6	2	31	96	17.04
5 Robos Revenge	4	2	1	18	96	9.68
6 Pasha Lass	3	4	6	10	96	3.22

Figure 38

'Likely to prove fruitful'

form that appear in the *Sporting Life*) to have taken part in real, as opposed to trial, races, since the times of the latter so often throw out, cloud or complicate your calculations of winning prospects.

If it is found that all the 24 races shown in the *Sporting Life*'s extensive form coverage of a race were graded (i.e. not trial or handicap) events and, provided the race in question is also covered in "Performance Pointers" and a further *Sporting Life* feature, the ratings service of "Clockwork" (this newspaper's watch-holding private handicapper), then the backer can reasonably assume that time and effort spent on further calculations are likely to prove fruitful.

An example of such an event run at Hackney (the principal and widely covered greyhound meeting on Thursday, 22 March 1990) appears in figure 35 together (in figures 36 and 37, *page 80 & 81*) with the ratings "Clockwork" accorded its runners and statistics relating to the career achievements of these as shown in the *Sporting Life*'s "Performance Pointers" feature.

As can be seen, the above table (figure 38, *page 82*) reflects the likelihoods that the trap allocated to a greyhound, its most recent race time and the speed with which it has run fastest to the first bend in its recent runs (which, if rapid, may well have propelled it clear of any interference at this trouble-fraught point) will have crucial effects on the outcome of a greyhound race.

As for the actual entries to be made into the first five columns of the above table, the first consists of information given in a feature supplied by "Clockwork" in the *Sporting Life* (see above). Most usefully, this expert assessor takes account of the advantage or otherwise that its allotment to a particular trap has accorded each dog running at the day's principal meeting.

First then, the "trap bonus" ratings "Clockwork" provided for the Hackney meeting held on the afternoon of Tuesday, 22 March 1990, were entered into the first column of the above table. This meant that, for example, Beggar's Ball received a top-rated score of six.

Next (as indicated in his formline) this runner, for having run his last race in a time of 32.88 seconds, which was second only to the fastest last time out

Recent placing achieved in any of greyhound's last four runs	Points to be awarded
Win in A1/M1/S1 race	24
Second in above grades	23
Third in above grades	22
Win in A2/M2/S2 race	21
Second in above grades	20
Third in above grades	19
Win in A3/M3/S3 race	18
Second in above grades	17
Third in above grades	16
Win in A4/M4/S4 race	15
Second in above grades	14
Third in above grades	13
Win in A5/M5/S5 race	12
Second in above grades	11
Third in above grades	10
Win in A6/M6/S6 race	9
Second in above grades	8
Third in above grades	7
Win in A7/M7/S7 race	6
Second in above grades	5
Third in above grades	4
Win in A8/M8/S8 race	3
Second in above grades	2
Third in above grades	1

Figure 39

'clocking' of Slanemore Rocket of 32.79, was credited with five points in the second column of the table whereas, here, in contrast, My Titan was only given one point, for having taken as long as 33.61 to last cover 523 yards.

Into the third column points should be entered that reflect the relative speeds at which the runners have advanced to the first bend in their last four races (as also shown in their *Sporting Life* form summaries). What you are rewarding most highly here is the dog that seems likely to be clear of any interference that may handicap its slower rivals as centrifugal force causes them to come together at the first bend – the point at which many races are either won or lost. This time the greyhound with the fastest of all the 24 or so first bend times shown in the *Sporting Life* should be awarded one point and the runner whose fastest previous run to the first bend is slower than that of any of its rivals should be accorded six points. Thus, in the example race under consideration, the former score was allotted to Robo's Revenge and the latter to Pasha Lass.

Next, and most crucially, a more complicated calculation needs to be performed to measure the class of any placings gained by a runner in its four most recent races. For each placing (either first, second or third) a dog has achieved in its last four races it is given points according to the following scale (see figure 39), which rewards such achievements more highly if they have been in high-class graded races.

It should be noted that points are given each and every time a greyhound can be seen from its four-race formline to have finished either first, second or third in any of the above grades, but not in any handicap or

Step 1 (utilising "Clock- work's" "trap suitability" rating)	Enter figure from the third column of "Clockwork's" feature (6 for Beggar's Ball)
Step 2 (rating most recent times)	Press + key Enter "rank order" score for times last time out (5 for Beggar's Ball)
Step 3 (rating speed to first bend)	Press − key Enter "rank order" score for fastest previous time to first bend (N.B. highest score = 1 for fastest time) (3 for Beggar's Ball) Press = key
Step 4 (first stage of rating the class of any placings in last four runs)	Press × key Enter score achieved for any placings in first three in last four runs (40 for Beggar's Ball) Press = key
Step 5 (second stage of rating the class of any placings in first three in last four runs)	Press × key Enter 100 Press ÷ key Enter maximum possible places score in last four races i.e. 96 in all cases (96 for Beggar's Ball)
Step 6 (arriving at a final rating)	Press = key Press √ key For greyhound's final rating (18.25 for Beggar's Ball)

Figure 40

trial events. The duly totalled "class placing" points should be entered in the fourth column of the table (which should be prepared prior to your calculation).

Finally, in the fifth column, the figure 96 is entered for each and every runner since this (as 4×24) represents the highest possible class-points total any greyhound could hypothetically and optimally have gained if it had most recently taken part in and won four A1 races.

By way of further example of what to enter in the last two columns of the table, Beggar's Ball would have received 12 points (for a win in grade M5) plus 10 more for a third in this grade, nine more for an M6 win and a further nine for a similar achievement, and so would have been awarded a total score of 40. This was the figure to enter into the table's penultimate column, while 96 appeared in its final one.

You should find prior completion of a table of ratings (as shown on page 82) makes it convenient to perform calculations on a standard calculator. The chart shown on page 87 is a reminder of how calculations should proceed so as to give each of the contestants in a systematically chosen race their first set of ratings.

This greyhound's rating of 18.25, in fact, placed him well clear of his rivals, as can be seen if figure 38 is again (see figure 41) displayed to allow the necessary calculations to be followed and checked.

Many backers may wish to make whatever grey-hound is top-rated their selection, after the above procedure has been followed, but those with more time available should complete a second table so as to facilitate the assessment of five more factors that

Dog number	Enter "Clockwork's" "trap suitability" rating	Enter points for most recent time	Enter speed to first bend rating	Enter class rating for any recent placings in last four runs	Enter 96 as optimum class rating for last four outings	Final rating after computing these figures
1 Beggar's Ball	6	5 for 32.88 secs	3 for 6.01 secs	40 (12+10+9+9)	96 (24×4)	18.25
2 Pound Foolish	2	3 for 33.23 secs	5 for 6.09 secs	0 (–)	96 (24×4)	—
3 My Titan	1	1 for 33.61 secs	4 for 6.08 secs	25 (8+7+10)	96 (24×4)	—
4 Slanemore Rocket	5	6 for 32.79 secs	2 for 6.01 secs (twice)	31 (10+10+11)	96 (24×4)	17.04
5 Robos Revenge	4	2 for 33.41 secs	1 for 6.00 secs	18 (9+9)	96 (24×4)	9.68
6 Pasha Lass	3	4 for 33.05 secs	6 for 6.13 secs	10 (9+1)	96 (24×4)	3.22

Figure 41

research has shown can also have a bearing on the outcomes of greyhound races. These are contestants' records in the grade of contest in which they are due to compete, their achievements when previously running from the traps allocated to them, the number of outings (the fewer the better) since they were last successful, and their overall wins-to-runs ratios.

Fortunately, the "Performance Pointers" table of statistics for the day's principal greyhound meeting published in the *Sporting Life*, allows the backer to assess rapidly and conveniently all of these often crucial factors, as can be seen from figure 42.

PERFORMANCE POINTERS

COMPUTED PERFORMANCES AT HACKNEY (since 1/1/88)

2.03 (484m A8)	Total W-R	Per cent	£1 Level Stake	Trap Record	A8 Races	Since Win
Trap 1 - IVY FRANCIS	2-15	13.3	- 7.50	1-7	0-0	3
Trap 2 - BLACK HANNAH	0-6	-	- 6.00	0-0	0-4	-
Trap 3 - HOWARDSTOWN GIRO	0-1	-	- 1.00	0-0	0-1	-
Trap 4 - ROAD TO CAHIR	0-5	-	- 5.00	0-2	0-5	-
Trap 5 - STRONG BELIEF	0-11	-	- 11-00	0-5	0-5	-
Trap 6 - DEMES PURSUIT	0-5	-	- 5.00	0-1	0-1	-
2.19 (484m A7)	Total W-R	Per cent	£1 Level Stake	Trap Record	A7 Races	Since Win
Trap 1 - JUMPING BING	3-22	13.6	- 5.75	3-14	2-10	7
Trap 2 - MONROE SLIPPER	0-2	-	- 2.00	0-0	0-0	-
Trap 3 - TRACTON DASHER	9-47	19.1	- 6.12	4-23	3-9	1
Trap 4 - HOWARDSTOWN BAND	1-3	33.3	- 0.75	1-2	0-2	1
Trap 5 - OYSTER NANCY	3-19	15.8	+ 1.25	2-7	1-9	3
Trap 6 - MICHAELS DOG	1-10	10.0	- 7.00	0-2	0-5	7
2.37 (523m M5)	Total W-R	Per cent	£1 Level Stake	Trap Record	M5 Races	Since Win
Trap 1 - BEGGARS BALL	7-40	17.5	- 11.50	2-5	1-18	0
Trap 2 - POUND FOOLISH	2-14	14.3	- 8.00	0-1	0-5	4
Trap 3 - MY TITAN	5-32	15.6	- 1.50	2-14	0-10	5
Trap 4 - SLANEMORE ROCKET	2-16	12.5	- 10.25	0-4	0-8	4
Trap 5 - ROBOS REVENGE	3-8	37.5	+ 6.50	1-4	0-0	0
Trap 6 - PASHA LASS	1-4	25.0	0.00	1-1	0-0	0
2.52 (484m A7)	Total W-R	Per cent	£1 Level Stake	Trap Record	A7 Races	Since Win

Figure 42

The rationale underpinning this second method of calculating the winning chance of greyhounds also involves the betting market. This is because it is often a crucial pointer to likely performance.

As can be seen from the table of ratings (figure 43), its initial column concerns a contender's position in either the *Sporting Life*'s betting forecast or, if you are at a meeting or in a betting shop, its position in the actual betting show. Thus Beggar's Ball, for figuring as the 6-4 forecast favourite in the *Sporting Life* of 22 March 1990, was accorded six points, while the complete outsiders, My Titan and Robos Revenge were each given one point. (It should be noted that generally betting forecasts are likely to feature entries for each runner that are far more differentiated than in figure 43.)

To make an entry into the second column of figure 44, information from the fifth column of the "Performance Pointers" feature has to be converted to a percentage. Thus, Beggar's Ball was given a score of five (rounded down from 5.51) for having (as indicated in the *Sporting Life*) won once in 18 attempts in A5 races.

In the table's third column, Beggar's Ball was also credited with a maximum low score of 0 having won last time out (as indicated by his "since win" statistic of 0) – a figure which was entered in the third column of the ratings table. Finally, his overall (7) wins to (40) runs ratio, as shown in the "Performance Pointers" table, was entered across the remaining two columns of the ratings table.

The figures from this table were duly entered into a standard calculator and featured in the same key-pressing sequence of steps (ending with the square-

2.37   (523 metres M5)   £44

Trap 1—BEGGARS BALL bk b Game Ball — Hollands Kay 2/87 (9/4/89) .... Maxen

Date											
20 Mr	523	1	6.10	1st	1¼	Easy Captain led run in	32.68	+20	7-2	M5	32.88
13 Mr	523	2	6.12	3rd	2½	Catch Lucky ev ch	32.56	+10	8-1	M5	32.86
10 Mr	523	1	6.10	1st	2	HIDE JET led run in	32.64	+20	7-2	M6	32.84
6 Mr	523	2	6.01	1st	Hd	Poor Old Fred fin well	32.75	+20	7-2	M6	32.95

Trap 2—POUND FOOLISH w bk b Ballregan Bob — Celtic Aran 2/88 .... Greenacre

Date											
20 Mr	523	3	6.09	5th	4¼	Beggars Ball b blk 1	32.68	+20	12-1	M5	33.23
13 Mr	523	3	6.17	5th	4½	Catch Lucky ev ch	32.56	+10	7-1	M5	33.02
8 Mr	523	3	6.12	4th	5¾	Hard To Live b crd to 1	32.38	+20	4-1	M5	33.05
1 Mr	523	3	6.27	5th	5¾	Clune Spinner ev ch	32.48	+10	7-4F	M5	32.96

Trap 3—MY TITAN w bk d Master Stack — Night Horizon 2/87 .... Walsh

Date											
13 Mr	523	4	6.25	2nd	2½	Robos Revenge wide 4 bmpd ran on ..	33.31	+10	11-8F	M6	33.61
6 Mr	523	3	6.08	3rd	3¼	Beggars Ball eased 3	32.75	+20	13-8F	M6	33.21
1 Mr	523	2	6.13	6th	4¾	Clune Spinner handy to 3	32.48	+10	10-1	M5	32.97
15 Fb	523	3	6.33	3rd	5¾	Dutchmans Nippy ev ch	32.84	-10	5-1	M5	33.20

Trap 4—SLANEMORE ROCKET (W) bd d Game Man — Munsboro Pa 4/87 .... Chandler

Date											
8 Mr	523	5	6.10	3rd	1½	Hard To Live ev ch	32.33	+20	9-4F	M5	32.79
3 Mr	523	6	6.15	5th	1½	Tomaroy Hall crd 1	32.93	+10	6-4F	M5	33.15
1 Mr	523	4	6.01	2nd	2¼	Clune Spinner q a led to 2	32.48	+10	4-1	M5	32.76
17 Fb	523	4	6.01	3rd	2¼	Tomaroy Hall showed to 3	32.73	-10	4-1	M5	32.82

Figure 43

Trap 5—ROBOS REVENGE (W) w bk d Sand Man — Andy's Lighthouse 5/87 .... Bateman

13 Mr	523 6	6.09	1st	2½	My Titan e p led 1	..............33.31	+10	5-1	M6	33.41
6 Mr	523 5	6.00	6th	10¼	Beggars Ball crd 1	..............32.75	+20	7-1	M6	33.77
20 Fb	523 4	6.04	4th	7¼	Easy Captain ev ch	..............33.00	-20	9-2	M6	33.38
13 Fb	523 5	5.87	1st DHT		Pound Foolish al led held on	..............33.09	N	8-1	M6	33.09

Trap 6—PASHA LASS (W) f b Whisper Wishes — Ballyhaden Queen 8/88 .... Tite

20 Mr	523 6	6.13	1st	Nk	Bob The Poacher wide led n/l	..............33.05	N	3-1	M6	33.05
13 Mr	523 5	6.16	4th	5	Robos Revenge b blk 1 and 4	..............33.31	+10	5-2	M6	33.81
6 Mr	523 5	6.14	4th	5½	Beggars Ball b blk 1	..............32.64	+20	9-2	M6	33.28
6 Mr	484 5	4.13	3rd	1½	Ardbeg Support s a ran on	..............30.49	+20	4-1	A8	30.81

BETTING: 6-4 Beggars Ball, 15-8 Slanemore Rocket, 6 Pound Foolish, Pasha Lass, 12 My Titan, Robos Revenge
Sel: BEGGARS BALL D.: Slanemore Rocket F.Alt: Pound Foolish

1 Beggars Ball—drawn well, quick double on the cards, stays
2 Pound Foolish—middle tracker, plenty of luck needed to score
3 My Titan—unimpressive in recent outings, runs on
4 Slanemore Rocket—push nose in front by the turn, has to be caught
5 Robos Revenge—loves to dictate, four likely to fill that roll
6 Pasha Lass—takes a step up in company after narrow victory, wide

Figure 43 (continued)

93

Greyhound's number and name	Points for position in betting	Wins in grade A5 as a percentage (rounded down if necessary)	Number of outings since last win	Overall wins to	Overall runs
1 Beggar's Ball	6	5 (from 5.51)	0	7	40
2 Pound Foolish	4	0	4	2	14
3 My Titan	2	0	5	5	32
4 Slanemore Rocket	5	0	4	2	16
5 Robos Revenge	2	0	0	3	8
6 Pasha Lass	4	0	0	1	4

Figure 44

root button) that have so often been adopted in many of the selection methods already described. This produced the following ratings:

Beggar's Ball	13.87
Pound Foolish	0
My Titan	0
Slanemore Rocket	3.53
Robos Revenge	8.66
Pasha Lass	10.00

Once the two sets of calculations were complete for the example race, Beggar's Ball emerged as the top-rated greyhound. Thus he became a nap selection and so carried a sizeable stake. He won, of course, at the surprisingly generous starting price of 7-4.

Postscript

By now it should be abundantly clear that the pocket calculator possesses a vast potential for winner-finding on the racecourse and at the greyhound track that few have dreamt of or appreciated.

Currently this potential is increasing as both horse- and dog-racing receive ever more sophisticated quantitative coverage. Rather than the often time-consuming and tedious task of inputting data into a computer to run a programme whose rationale and precise workings remain a mystery, the racing enthusiast who takes up "button pressing" on a pocket calculator has work to do that he or she is likely to find absorbingly pleasant, easy to perform and, above all, potentially profitable.

Indeed, when the results of races are seen to confirm prior calculations – as in the many examples contained in this book – you are likely to experience immense satisfaction and delight.